AF241804

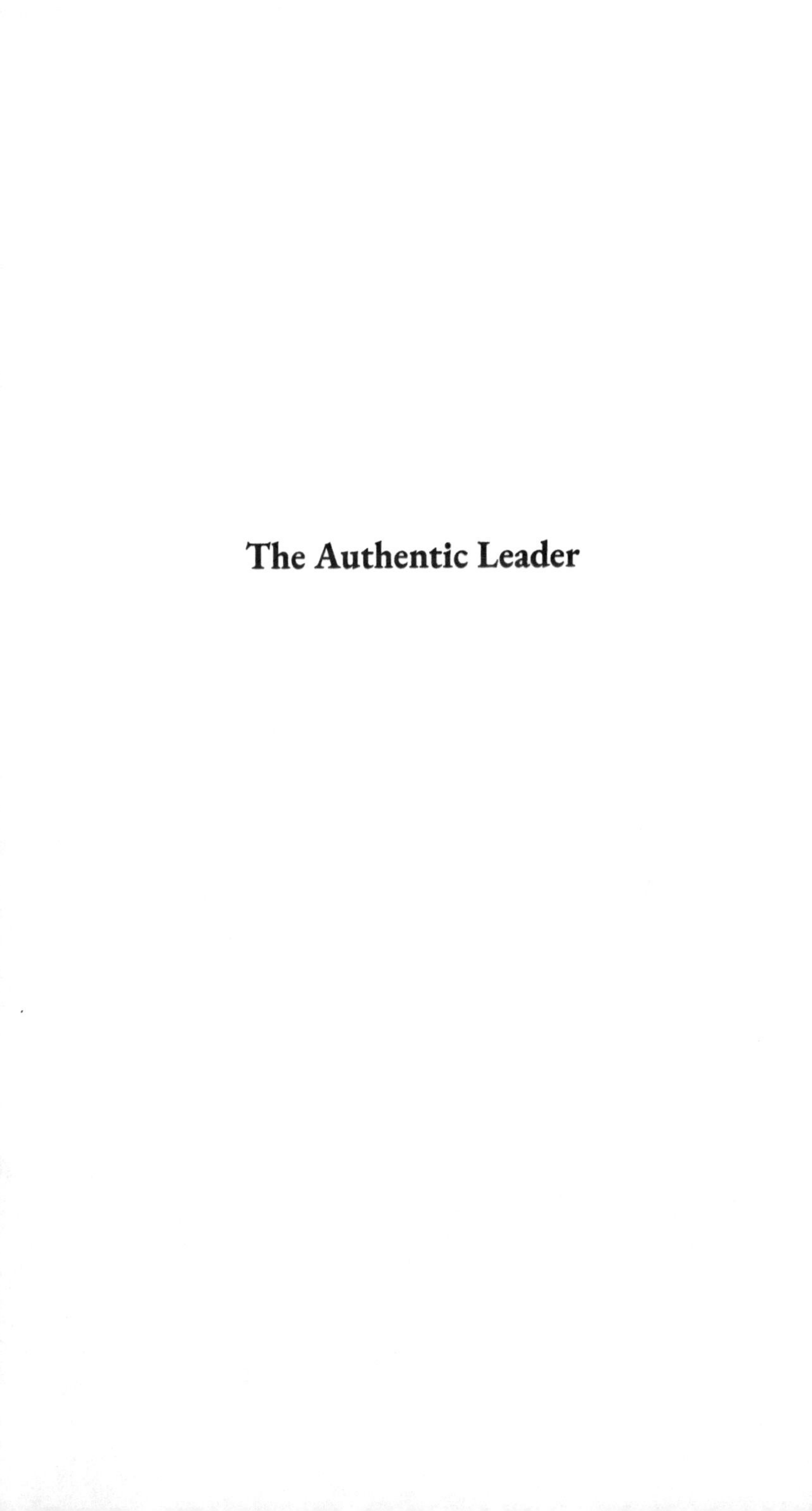

The Authentic Leader

The Authentic Leader

a guide to knowing yourself and being courageous

Dominique Stillman

Head 4 Leadership Publishing

First published in 2026 by Head 4 Leadership Publishing

ISBN (paperback): 978-1-9195600-0-7
ISBN (e-book): 978-1-9195600-1-4

Cover Design: Dan Cooper

Dedication

This book is dedicated to

Albi and Leo, my smart and wonderful preschool grandsons.

Foreword

'Dominique's book provides practical, timely insights that today's leaders can actually use. I'm thrilled to see the ripple effects of neuroscience education shaping this work.'

Dr Sarah McKay, Neuroscientist, Creator of the Neuroscience Academy and Author of *Brain Health for Dummies* and *The Women's Brain Book*

Contents

Introduction

'I don't know what happened in that meeting. I felt so pressured. I said nothing, despite wanting to.'

Faced with the considerable expectations that arise with progression into management and leadership roles, phrases like this one above often come up with my coaching clients.

In trying to meet expectations, you can feel like you're an imposter, feel overwhelmed, or see yourself as 'out of your league' with peers and others. You judge yourself harshly. You think that to be successful in meeting your responsibilities, and achieving the potential that others have seen, you need to be someone you think you're not!

THE GOOD NEWS is that this is you being authentic! This is what you feel at that time, in that moment. These feelings of doubt, or of being *less than*, aren't pleasant ones and are often driven by fears, both known and unknown. The same applies if you come from the following perspective, 'This is me, take it or leave it,' which can be a defensive, self-protective standpoint.

MORE GOOD NEWS is that exploring what's behind your thoughts and feelings, increasing your self-awareness and managing or overcoming your fears and concerns is your route to becoming even more authentic, which makes for a positive impact as a leader.

Some of this book is for new and aspiring leaders, those of you who have not yet, perhaps, fully appreciated and valued your strengths, your purpose and what you stand for. There's also a fantastic opportunity here for established leaders who might, regardless of your experience, have dips in your confidence and self-belief. You are human after all! Others in influential positions may also find this book useful. The solicitor, executive assistant or account manager for example.

I'm writing this, so that *you* can be part of the creation and spread of a healthy workplace culture. One where you lead and model to bring out others' courage, resilience and compassion. One where working with you and for you, is a trusted space even in the tough times. Where fear and its toxic impact can be dismissed.

Having been a leadership coach for decades and having worked across many industries and for a fair few leaders myself, *and* having studied human behaviour, I've used this and other first-hand experience to inform the content.

Such study has included neuroscience and brain health, which is now an integral part of my leadership coaching practice – a healthy mindset makes for better decisions and working environments. Here you'll find insights and ideas that will help you in terms of clear thinking and being courageous, even when the situation is challenging.

There will also be reference to well-tested leadership models and tools that can give structure to how you work on a daily basis, including motivating, critiquing and influencing. A caveat here: leaders need to get results, which sometimes means tough decisions and conversations. Being authentic recognises and acknowledges that for some, leading isn't or is no longer right for them.

Thank you for choosing this book. Some of it may resonate now, some further along the road, and some parts, perhaps not at all. That's fine. My hope is that, as you progress, you'll acknowledge your feelings and reactions, look into them and gain more insight e.g. who you are, why you lead as you do and how you want to develop as a leader.

This is how you'll become even more authentic in your role. Leading doesn't require a title. Leading comes from how you are 'being'!

Dominique

The Leadership Challenge Index

Each chapter covers multiple situations that will benefit from the opportunity to be professionally authentic and courageous. In case you want to jump to a particular area that's on your mind, this map is here to help.

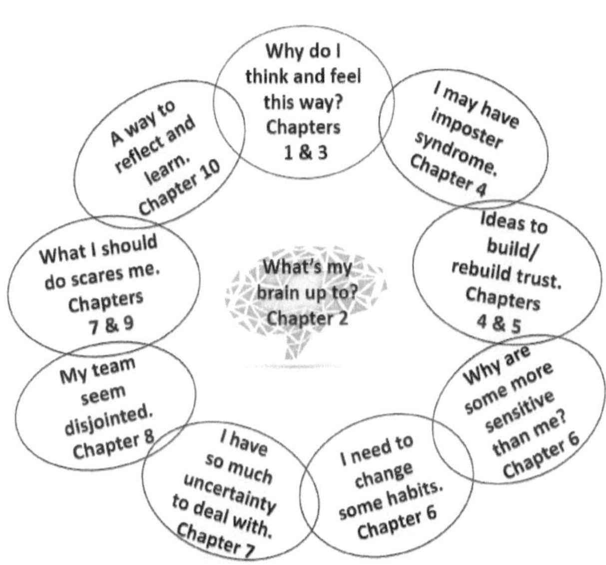

Chapter 1
My Story, What's Yours?

Have you ever done something that took you completely by surprise? When you became someone you didn't recognise as you?

The first time this happened to me was when I was walking home from school with a couple of other girls. I was about twelve, a polite smiley child. Often in the background, self-conscious and awkward in groups. Easily forgettable, to be honest.

That day, the three of us walked next to each other, me in the middle, one near the curb and the other near the gardens. The garden-side girl was becoming increasingly grating. For some reason, every time she spoke, she shoved my shoulder with her hand: *'You know what I mean,'* shove, *'Shall we go via the scary house?'* shove, and on it went. I didn't feel that she was being nasty and the shoves weren't particularly hard, but it was constant, increasingly annoying and not something she usually did.

'Can you not shove me please?' I said. Then it happened again! So, I said to her, *'If you do that again, I'm*

going to shove you back.' This was the first time I'd been that straightforward or clear, outside of my sibling relationships.

She shoved me again, this time with a glint in her eye, as if to check that I'd meant what I'd said. So, I turned to face her and with both hands pushed her with enough force to send her flying over a garden wall and into some rose bushes. '*I asked you not to.*' I said and walked off.

While she was dusting herself down, I walked on, wondering what had happened to me. The strength of my actions surprised me. I'd scared myself – I wasn't someone who pushed people around. I was more likely to smile and ignore something bothering me, or to move away from a situation that made me uncomfortable. I didn't confront people, as I felt unable to deal with any unpleasant repercussions. In that moment, I felt ashamed of my behaviour and resolved that if losing my temper led to such (physical) behaviour, I needed to curb it. It wasn't that I didn't fight with my brother (he was nearest in age to me) or argue with my elder sisters, but I was brought up not to behave like that in public.

My upbringing was in most aspects very happy. You might think that as my parents were well-read, well-travelled, independent and frequently engaged in political and religious debate, especially over the washing up on Sundays, that I'd be comfortable with challenge and disagreement. Not so. Manners mattered greatly, respect for elders was important, you didn't speak until you were spoken to and you ate what you were given, to name just a few of the rules we lived by.

But, socialising outside of the family, as a child, is one of the greatest ways to understand and learn from others. It's where you can gather ideas and resources for navigating new situations and dealing with different types of people and behaviour.

School was the first time I spent extended time with other children: it was daunting. Also, I didn't get to go to Brownies or ballet like my elder sisters, because they dropped out and so it was assumed that I would too. My younger brother did Cubs and football and I felt overlooked sometimes.

Being able to articulate, debate intelligently and be well-read was something that my dad, especially, valued. Both parents were lifelong informal learners. Despite this, I can't recall conversations with them about ambitions or careers. University was not mentioned, and my school did very little to inspire me in terms of work and life opportunities. Regarding my parents, we were expected to have left home and be looking after ourselves by the age of 21. We all had.

As a result, I was great at being what I thought they wanted, and unpractised at expressing myself freely. If I said something that wasn't 'correct', invited or clear, it might be met with *'Don't they teach you anything at school?'*, *'Learn to annunciate,'* or *'Shh'*. Being quiet, seemed a good option to avoid their criticism and my embarrassment.

More importantly, I was also unrehearsed in understanding what feelings and emotions are, and how to use them well. This has become a key part of my work with leaders. And, those leaders, like me, have benefitted from increasing their emotional knowledge and management, their *emotional intelligence* (see Daniel Goleman).

Fast forward to my teenage years where shyness and awkwardness prevailed. Inside, I had a burning desire to commit to ideas and experiences but was overwhelmed by nerves and fear of rejection or ridicule. School had been hard from a friendship perspective: I wasn't bullied but I was often on the outer edge of events, as I wasn't local to the schools I attended and I changed schools in my teens to one my parents felt was better. I had no idea who I was, or what I wanted or didn't want out of life. This became a problem, because it meant I put others' needs ahead of checking in with what mine might be.

I left school with average results and a desperate need to get away from the discomfort of the school environment. As noted earlier, university wasn't discussed as a choice by my parents (my elder sisters went straight into work) and it wasn't pushed by my school either. And at that time, I couldn't wait to get away from education.

Having met a very motivated guy through my first job, we got together. I was inspired by his dream and drive to be a millionaire business owner. His aspirational route started via the place where we both worked, a petrol station.

The idea was to get our own franchised petrol station, but we needed savings to do this. So, we lived off my wages and saved his from his area manager role.

Aged nineteen and twenty-two, we got our first franchise! We then began working towards and living *his* dream and for a long time I was happy to go along with this. I soon learnt about managing income and outgoings and building relationships with our suppliers and customers. I also learnt about displaying products and dealing with petrol and diesel deliveries. I discovered I was very good with people in general and customers in particular.

One day I mentioned that I'd quite like a business of my own. It was a spoken thought that hadn't been explored more deeply. I hadn't got to the point of knowing what type of business it would be, just that, having supported his dream, maybe there was something that would be of more interest to me.

A few weeks later my partner presented me with some keys. He'd bought me a shop that sold car stereos, aerials and sunroofs, something I knew nothing about and had never shown any interest in!

At 21 years old I was left to run the shop while he ran the petrol station and other businesses. It included staff who hadn't known the shop had been sold, so they were really happy – not! There was a client list of car showrooms that would come to us to have stereos or sunroofs fitted as part of their sales service, as well as walk-in customers. I was completely out of my depth but, as it was now in our name, I felt I had to be committed to making it work.

It was the hardest transition I've had to deal with and the stress was extreme. I was still a fairly shy, naïve young woman. The people who now worked for me were, thankfully, kind: they came with me to client meetings and showed me how to fit stereos, aerials and sunroofs. Not that I'd do this regularly, but it meant that I could talk more knowledgeably (or bluff less) to clients. I watched the team talk about our products with walk-in shoppers and copied this when I was alone with them.

Because of the hours we worked – seven days for the garage (7am to 11pm) and six days for the shop (9am to 5pm) – my partner and I didn't have time to talk about us and our individual needs. I wasn't versed in any form of leadership or management development. I didn't reflect on what I was doing or why I was doing it. I just did what I thought was right at the time. It wasn't always right.

After a couple of years, we sold the shop – it came with a flat and that created a decent profit on the deal. We also changed petrol stations and then we bought another franchise, this time a fashion outlet selling ties and men's accessories. I was to run this, while my partner ran the petrol station and managed the refurbishment of properties that had also been acquired. His drive was unrelenting.

There was so much to deal with, that the doubts and concerns I had were pushed down. We continued to buy and sell properties and also took on two pub franchises. For many years we did well, financially. For what though? We didn't have holidays, we rarely saw each other, and we failed to discuss with each other how we felt about things, such as why we were doing what we were doing and the challenges of running these businesses. It was lonely, but family and friends thought we were amazing!

We worked, I'm not going to say together, but in co-ownership for ten years, but eventually we and the business came to an unglamourous end.

What I failed to master was that I mattered to me. That all the 'doing' was hiding feelings and frustrations and preventing opportunities to address concerns.

I hadn't learnt that the girl who'd pushed someone over the wall had been (clumsily) expressing her feelings and was determined to make herself heard. A fleeting moment that my 12-year-old head perceived to be unhelpful could have been fine-tuned and developed.

Most of us are not taught at school about emotions: how to recognise them and make them work for us. We're also not educated on how to reflect on our thinking processes and challenge them. We're rarely tutored about what resilience is and how to build it. Did anyone impart thinking and ideas, for coming back from mistakes or handling difficulties, with you? You may have been lucky and had a mentor, teacher, family member or friends to stir this awareness. Such tutoring helps reveal and fine-tune the you inside, the leader inside, and enables authentic relationships that are critical to business success.

My route to self-knowing took a while and I hope this book can speed the process up for you. When my business partnership ended after ten years, I had nothing to show for it materially. No home (I'd lived in one of the pubs) and no money: the recession of the early 1990's left huge debts. My parents sold their house to help with the debts, and the guilt and shame I felt, due to them having to move because of me, was mental torture.

I was exhausted from the stress and had so little confidence that one day I couldn't even decide which pair of socks to put on, in case I got it wrong! With the mental pain came physical pain, headaches, insomnia and nausea.

Despite this, getting a 'real' job was top of my mind. I got a Yellow Pages business directory (I'm showing my age here – this was pre-internet), started at A and found airlines, then under B, I found British Airways. After a phone call, interviews and assessment centre visits I became a part-time check in agent.

Survival mode was a state I unconsciously remained in for too long. It was a state of prolonged stress. A state where my entire focus was on working hard, diluting the guilt and getting a level of financial security once more. There was no time or space given to relaxing. However, as a leader, preparing for tough times and building your mental toughness can help you to navigate the difficulties when they do arise.

Ten years after I'd lost those businesses, I was working for a finance firm, in organisational development. I was supporting a group of managers who were being made redundant. By then I'd been a department manager at BA (leading an operations team), then shifted into people development at another organisation. Through a fabulous mentor, I gathered coaching and psychometric certifications. I honed my skills in designing training, facilitating and coaching nationally and internationally. I showed these soon-to-be-made-redundant managers the psychological impact of change, helping them with their emotional journey and providing strategies and tools to handle their redundancy situation. One day, as I talked them through the Kübler Ross model (the five stages of grief), I had a light bulb moment. I was okay. I'd been okay for years, I was financially secure, and yet I hadn't realised!

It was only then, after ten years in 'survival mode', that I began to share my experience and the lessons that could be learnt about hardiness and how to build it.

Business ownership and taking a leading role can be tough, although sometimes we make it tougher than it needs to be. Having studied neuroscience and brain health with Dr Sarah McKay, and followed that with neuroscience for coaching, I was driven to share those insights to enable leaders to be better and quicker at adapting to their situations.

Survival mode, and the focus it energises, has its place in the short term but being able to calm yourself (and others) will help you spot and traverse difficulties more quickly, and with less fallout (mental and physical). I've discovered how mental toughness is determined in part through personality, along with environmental experience (simplistically, nature plus nurture). Having developed my own mental toughness, the authentic self I now present is more direct: I say what I think and share my vulnerability appropriately.

Reflection Exercise

The neuroscience of memory is that your brain references your past and how you've recorded happenings. This is then used, unconsciously, to inform how you respond to future situations.

For example – As a child, I sometimes felt overlooked (e.g. not being able to do ballet), and that I didn't matter as much as the others. This carried forward into future situations, where I didn't speak up or stand up for myself. Understanding your unconscious reasoning is incredibly important in finding out who you are 'being' each day. Are you being a person from the past, who could be much more effective and 'real' today and for the future?

Try the following:

1. Write or record a summary of your upbringing. Just write – don't correct, reword or judge what comes up.

2. Read or listen back to it and notice the tone you've set, the language, the thoughts, the feelings and the definitions you've linked to that upbringing.

3. Notice what beliefs you have of yourself, about what your work is or isn't, about what success is and who you want acknowledgment from, etc.

4. How has your story shaped your values – how you make choices and decisions and what matters to you?

5. Notice how you deal with work situations today and what, from your back story, is playing out in today's world.

Note – whatever you learn isn't wrong or right: it's a chance to increase awareness and insight and gain greater consciousness. It also gives you opportunities to adjust and update how you have recorded your past.

For example: My not going to ballet wasn't only because my sisters dropped out, it was because money was tight and getting back and forth was difficult without transport. I can believe it was because I didn't matter or I can update that belief to having parents who were juggling priorities and doing their best, and that most of the time I was much loved and cared about. This adjustment and update of this memory (and others) reduced the impact of my nine-year-old self's influence on my adult view of the world. Leaders would do well to check in with their past (their story) and review its influence on how they act today.

Chapter 2
Some Neuroscience Insights

There is much out there about neuroscience, the subject has become much more commonly referred to. I became intrigued, as some of what I was hearing and reading seemed too good to be true. I took up studying this subject in 2016 and soon realised that some of what's talked about *is* too good to be true. I saw an advert that suggested a golf club could change your brain! I was certified in Applied Neuroscience and Brain Health by 2019, taking these studies further into 2021 through the Neuroscience Coaching Network.

My reason for going deeper into the subject? To provide clients with hidden insights into how and why they think, do and feel as they do. So that, with this knowledge, and with other tools, they could choose how to develop and be even better and more impactful.

This subject also drew me closer to understanding resilience and mental toughness. Something I also explore with my coaching clients.

In this section you will find three aspects of neuroscience, and life examples to demonstrate them. These aim to prompt your self-learning and create awareness of how this learning can be used with those you lead.

The intention is to give you, as leaders, insight into your mind's workings and what to expect from the other human minds you lead. Throughout this chapter and the rest of this book symbols will used at various points.

You'll find:

This symbol (above) for **an example**

This one (above) for the **neuroscience**

This one (above) for **ideas, questions and applications of the subject in discussion**

At the end of each chapter, you'll have already seen the symbol above to denote additional space for **notes and reflections**.

To get the most out of these next few pages, take part in, and explore yourself in the areas covered. Also, if possible, talk through the different parts with a trusted person who can question and appropriately challenge what comes up.

Some Neuroscience Insights

1. Minds make stuff up!

I was walking to school one day with a friend. It was a mile or so, and there was a big junction to traverse. On this occasion, we could see some emergency vehicles ahead. As we approached and crossed at the traffic lights, we saw that a bus (which we knew came from our right), had stopped in the middle. A car was nose-to-nose with it and a bicycle was on its side. Uniformed police were directing traffic and seeing to those on the bus and the other vehicles. A man with his back to us was being tended to by a paramedic. We didn't linger, but it was an unusual and dramatic scenario. On arriving at school my friend was eager to share with others what we had seen. I listened bemused!

'Well, this car jumped the traffic lights to make a right turn from the post office side, while from the sweet shop side the bus tried to avoid it and in doing so hit a cyclist! There was blood everywhere and the cyclist looked sickly pale!'

As our other friends asked for more details and expressed their curiosity at this rare excitement in a usually bland walk to school, my friend responded with confidence.

Reflecting on this as an adult I find it particularly interesting how easily my friend was believed, and also that my friend believed her own story!

Neuroscience – your brain is constantly predicting

Your brain's primary role is to protect you and guide you safely as you move through life. It is anticipating risk. Your brain does this using data collated over time and stored as memories. These include your energy needs, knowledge, values, experiences and relationships, as well as how they have impacted you emotionally. In milliseconds, and without conscious effort, your brain has steered your perspective and reactions.

Gaps in information are commonplace in all aspects of life. For the brain, though, uncertainty is a stressor. As your brain's role, at its most basic level, is to keep you alive, and to help humanity as a whole to continue (reproduction), new situations and unknowns stimulate attention; and an unconscious process of sifting through what you know or believe. This analysis is used to 'predict' the missing parts and potential risks. These educated guesses are not always correct! – as the example indicates.

This process includes an unconscious and millisecond threat assessment, which can raise or reduce uncertainty and generate actions and responses. Stress levels rise when certainty can't be found or the situation is perceived as threatening to something a person values. 'Finding' an explanation even if it's scary feels better than unknowns (even when the 'finding' is incorrect).

Leaders who provide clarity and certainty, positively impact morale, performance and wellbeing.

Leadership ideas to reduce ambiguity and strengthen relationships

You decide – would you rather your team 'guessed' what you meant or were expecting? Or, that you provided ways to create and give them greater transparency and certainty?

- I don't know many people who are psychic! It really is best to avoid assuming or presuming. Ask what has been understood to nip misconceptions in the bud. Enquire into concerns and follow up if none are shared immediately. Often these are not clear to people at the time

- Take more moments to put yourself in the shoes of others and anticipate as many of the questions, challenges or ideas that a new situation could raise (this is empathy in practice). This helps you to prepare what you communicate more thoroughly, AND reduces the chances of you being taken by surprise by the questions or feedback

- Provide multiple methods for checking what people are thinking and feeling in team meetings and on an individual basis

- Listen out for, and be connected to, the rumour mill, so that you can immediately correct or update where misunderstandings are being shared. This can involve addressing specific people or as a general update. Maybe both!

In my leadership roles I found that regularly 'walking the floor', in person or virtually, seeing how people were, was one of the most useful ways for me to stay connected. It gave me an opportunity to update, learn, correct and, above all, strengthen trust.

2. Brains love habits

A colleague once told me about a time after they'd moved house. A few weeks later, the person was driving home after work, and it was only when they pulled up outside that they realised they'd gone to the old house!

You might have a friend who is a full-on gym bunny and becomes openly distressed if they can't keep to their fitness routine, sessions and classes.

If your mobile phone plays up or gets broken, or you've left it behind, what does it feel like?

There are so many things that we do without thinking, and habits we have adopted like relying on our mobile phones.

Because habits (thoughts and behaviours) are unconscious, they impact every part of your life, including how you lead. Why is that and how?

Neuroscience – habits require repetition

Because your brain is always on, different parts of your brain are continuously communicating with each other, until you die. Habits require less conscious effort and less energy – allowing your brain to save energy for the times when it has to be alert, when there are surprises that haven't been predicted.

A habit is a collection of behaviours or brain activity. A repeated action, thought and feeling connected to a situation becomes a habit. Like a muscle that gets stronger when exercised, habit wiring is strengthened by repetition. The result is that the habit response becomes so fast, it's automatic, often unconscious and requires less energy. Habits are not dissimilar to addictions, which means that some are good for us and some less so.

One of the brain chemicals associated with habit formation is dopamine. Dopamine is a reward chemical, triggered when something you have done makes you feel good, as it creates relief and, or, a pleasant emotional response. This stimulates you to repeat that something. As this continues, dopamine is triggered *in anticipation* of reward and so motivates repeated behaviour.

For example, you are stuck in traffic. A passenger suggests a way around the jam that is new to you. You take up their suggestion and success; you are not delayed. This new route and how it has saved you time makes you feel triumphant (dopamine)!

On another day, you recall the route and give it another go, you gain satisfaction from remembering and it works for you once more. Feeling gleeful and satisfied are because dopamine, that feel-good hormone has been released. Your brain seeks to feel good (which means safe and secure), so next time you are driving in the area you unconsciously, 'anticipate' the benefit of taking the new route (that's the dopamine again), and the route becomes your new habit.

Habits don't disappear, although they may become less important as newer habits begin to dominate. That's not to say that an old habit, won't reappear! This is normal. Not all habits are good for us, even if they make us 'feel' good in the short term. Overindulging in unhealthy food can be delightful in the moment but can also quickly trigger regret.

Leadership habits

You decide – let habits go unchecked or gain clarity on habits and put your efforts into the most effective ones?

- What can you identify as your unhelpful leadership habits? What could you change in how you act and behave, and what would be the reward (feeling and benefit) for doing so?

- What strong habits can you adopt and demonstrate that create a positive culture and an example of consistency and reliability for others to replicate?

- If habits are stimulated by the reward (dopamine), based on anticipation of an action or behaviours outcomes, what recognition are you giving to your team's positive efforts and outcomes? For example, where you see collaboration or increased customer satisfaction and acknowledge that, to encourage more

- Recognition and encouragement can aid the best practice and behaviour of your team members. What habits can you have in place to provide this recognition appropriately?

3. Brains: a short guide to their inner workings and how to maximise them!

Think about a time when you'd had a fabulous day! You felt great, perhaps you did things you found interesting or spent time with people who made you feel good. Within that day you may have had some complicated things to deal with, and you handled them well. Even if the day wasn't wholly successful you felt positive as you went to bed that night. What contributed to this day being fabulous?

Consider now a horrible day. A day not vastly different from another and yet you felt tense, what you had to do was frustrating, the people around you seemed irritating, and your patience was low. Even if not totally unsuccessful as a day, you went to bed that night feeling fed up. What contributed to that day being horrible?

Neuroscience – the interplay of biology, psychology and sociology

Whether you have a good or a bad day, looking at the interplay of the Bottom-Up, Outside-In, Top-Down (bio-psycho-social) model has been one of the ways my coaching clients have been able to understand some of why they behave as they do, think as they think and feel as they feel.

A three-way bio-psycho-social model
adapted from Sarah McKay PhD, *Brain Health for Dummies*

Reflecting on the model's three parts, can help you ascertain what influenced the way you interpreted how a day turned out (successful/unsuccessful)? The model can also be used to spot and make useful adjustments, that can help you set yourself up better for future days and events.

Bottom-Up – Take control of your nutrition and the fuel intake that works for you as a whole person. Prioritise sleep, space for exercise, time to rest to oil the mechanics of your brain and body.

Some physical and mental health conditions develop or are part of your makeup, but they will always benefit from a healthy diet, quality sleep and exercise. The inner workings of the brain and body functions, and how you care for them, directly influence your mood and actions as a leader, manager and business owner.

There is so much out there, and many experts to help with the 'Bottom-Up' aspect of your brain. Diet experts, sleep experts, hormone experts and exercise experts. To name but a few.

Your brain is constantly monitoring the resources it has, to enable the body to respond to life situations. The fuel and care you provide directly impacts not just how your body functions but also the quality of your thinking. Teams, colleagues, and customers deserve quality thinking, don't they?

Top-Down – Notice the way you describe your life. What are the strong memories and life experiences that come out when you talk about your life? What emotions and feelings are connected to the actions and reactions contained in your narratives of your life's experiences?

Your brain uses these versions of your life, subconsciously, as reference points for how you perceive, approach and conduct yourself in any situation. Including how you make decisions and judgements.

Inspect these stories, understand them and the perspective you present through them. How are they aiding or hindering you as you lead others?

For example, when I was at school and was about six, there was a girl in my class who I decided wasn't nice. I have no recollection of why I thought she wasn't nice. Her name was Liz. For years, if I heard of, or met someone with the name Liz, I imagined the person wouldn't be pleasant to know. My brain had put some events and feelings together, prompting a belief that people called Liz are unpleasant! Ridiculous, I know. For a six-year-old, though, being wary of Liz's was a good plan, so my brain could keep me safe – its primary role.

For years, hearing or reading about that name prompted an immediate, subtle emotional response of wariness. As an adult, though, once I had met some other Liz's in person, that unconscious response was put to bed.

Sometimes we can hear our 'mind talk' from our 'Top-Down' perspective, that inner voice that creates doubts and other immediate thought responses. This voice is compiled from beliefs constructed from our life experiences and environments. For example, a religious upbringing can create voices that judge through that religious lens, what you can and cannot do; and what you think others should or shouldn't do.

Life experiences trigger some of our ways of being and leading. Inspection of these can help you to revisit your brain's 'data base' and update your interpretation of events to be more suitable for your life today and your leadership role and responsibilities.

Outside-In – Would you agree that who and what you connect with, and the things and situations you immerse yourself in create a way of being and feeling? Being in like-minded groups matters to the brain. Your social brain is vital: we all need others at various points in our lives, and to varying degrees, for us to get on (or survive). You are, have been or will be part of some clubs, teams, friendships, study groups and family. Those groups and other interests you nurture, stimulate how you think and feel about life, work and other subjects.

The social groups, social media platforms, where you get your news and how you challenge or inspect the 'outside' information you connect to, influence how you feel and see the world.

To complete the Neuroscience Coaching Network certification, I was part of a group who researched the social brain (part of Outside-In) and the impact of lone working. Within that research – *'in total, in Great Britain, 33% of adults feel occasionally, sometimes or often lonely. This equates to over 25 million people.'*

A sense of isolation, loneliness and feeling you don't matter to others is detrimental to mental health. *'Loneliness can be described as a subjective perception of being stranded, abandoned or cutoff. It is where closeness, trust, affection, love and community are deemed missing. It isn't automatically associated to being on one's own.' (Dr Sarah McKay, Neuroscientist)*

Leaders with awareness of this dial up personal connections with all their team members, regardless of their working arrangements.

Leadership with the brain in mind

You decide – you can focus just on the work and results, or you can focus on creating a connected team who share and safely challenge their thinking. A team who positively impacts and supports each other.

- As a leader, you are an 'Outside-In' to others. How is your way of leading helping your team to be their best? What experiences and knowledge are you sharing to broaden resources? When has it been tough emotionally for you as a leader? What was behind that and what ways did you find to overcome it?

- Everyone's biology is different and there are times when this becomes challenging for people – how will you spot this in yourself, and also enable your team to have what they need to function well (e.g. lunch, rest, exercise)?

- Life experiences generate beliefs and emotions. What stresses you? What motivates you? Do you know the answer to these questions for those in your team? How can you learn from each other, and broaden your perspectives and insights?

- Stress is a part of life, but sustained stress will have performance consequences for you and your team. Do you know what situations, people and work create stress in yourself and for your team?

- Team development sessions highlight differences, strengths and ways to work better together. Are you enabling regular space for these?

To conclude, I have found that neuroscience has a special place when applied to how you lead. So much of what you think and do is unconsciously driven by your brain's requirement to save energy for when you most need it. Your self-awareness and introspection helps you to redress out of date beliefs, and to create new habits that can override older ones.

In my coaching work, many of my clients reveal habits and beliefs that stem from childhood and teenage years. When I say to clients, '*I think you are letting a ten-year-old make decisions for you.*' they realise the value of this self-awareness.

Your ideas and actions

Chapter 3
Emotions: how are you feeling?

'Don't get emotional' is a phrase I've sometimes heard directed at myself and at others. In person, and in books, films, etc, the display of emotions, especially where they are linked to fear and sadness, can be portrayed as negative, even as a sign of weakness.

This misconception does a great disservice to the real and vital purpose of emotions, moods and feelings. The reason this subject gets its own chapter is because every part of your life is linked to an emotion or to an emotional response (a feeling).

'It's nothing personal,' is another commonly heard expression that prefaces an often-unpleasant message. For example: 'It's not personal, it's a business decision that unfortunately your role is no longer required.'

Leading on from the previous chapter on neuroscience, and the role of memory and prediction in how you decipher the world, here I'll explain how *everything* is connected to emotions and therefore can feel personal. Awareness of this and why, can go a long way towards helping you to display your feelings in a manner that recognises you as a strong and compassionate leader, manager or business owner.

Emotions can be tricky if you see them as problems, rather than as valuable, natural and human indicators of your own state. What you feel can be considered as data that informs you how to respond.

In this chapter, I'm inviting you to expand your understanding of emotions and look at ways to increase your emotional language and emotional intelligence (EQ). I'm also inviting you to apply this in how you lead, how you manage your emotional responses and to have a positive impact on others. As a leader, mastering your responses to emotions can keep you in the right mindset for effectively handling the tough situations and decisions you have to deal with.

Currently, thankfully, sharing vulnerabilities appropriately is growing to be seen as a strength. A strength that allows you to be authentic and effective in your leadership behaviour.

As I mentioned in my introduction, what you feel is authentic to you at that moment. But as you will see in this chapter, you have agency over your feelings and this is where you can use feelings to stay calm, have clear thinking and reveal the authenticity that emerges from within that calmer state.

Noticing and describing how you feel

Some neuroscience – the part of your brain that handles language is not linked to the part that handles feelings, which is why we can't always describe how we feel when we're in a highly emotional state.

Have you noticed how, for example, when an athlete has a microphone in their face directly after winning a race, and is asked, 'How do you feel?' or 'What does this mean to you?' the reply might be, 'I can't find the words.' or 'I can't think right now?' The same applies at times of both joy and sadness.

It can take a moment for emotions to settle and gain calmness, in order to be able to find some words.

Let's get a bit of clarity on some of the words I've used.

Emotions – Are instinctive, subconscious, an immediate physiological, automatic response to something. An emotion is a hard-wired reaction, and part of the brain's protective mechanism, e.g. 'jumping' at the sound of a loud bang. Emotions are short (about 90 seconds), sharp and intense

Feelings – Are a person's conscious, psychological interpretation of that emotional reaction. Let's take the example of the loud bang which makes you jump – this is a protective response to a potential risk.

- This 'bang' creates a psychologically generated feeling, due to your personality, beliefs, values, memories and experiences. In this example, two people might both 'jump' at the same loud bang. One might then 'feel' intrigued to find out what caused it, while the other 'feels' scared and a need to get away. The duration of these feelings is more consciously influenced and can be held on to or changed through cognitive choice. Using another example, it can look like this

- You're working from home and your internet goes down. This infuriates you – you miss an important online call. When it comes back on, you're still annoyed, and it's on your mind for the rest of the day.

Or

- You're working from home and the internet goes down so you miss the online call. You feel frustrated! When it comes back on, you let everyone know, you tell them you hope the call went well without you and ask for an update. You then park it; it's one of those things. You *choose* to carry on with your day feeling engaged with what else needs to be done

Moods – Being in a good mood, bad mood, low mood, or being moody (switching back and forth) are states of being that can be harder to pin down as to how they've come about. They are often influenced by a combination of feelings, environments, and sometimes physical elements, such as hormones or pain. Moods are longer lasting (hours, days, weeks or months)

Self-awareness, a spotlight on feelings

Let's experiment: Since you got up this morning how many feelings have you noticed in yourself? Try listing them and what was happening during the first couple of hours of your day. To help you, here's a grid (below) and I've included a couple of examples. Some of the commonest emotions people refer to are listed. You can add others to suit.

Happy – Sad – Fear – Anger – Surprise – Disgust

What was happening (when)?	What was I feeling?	Why did I feel that way?
6am Alarm goes off – no sign of sun, again!	AGITATED and SLUGGISH	It's been five consecutive days of gloom! I miss the sun desperately!
6.15 am Exercise time	DREAD then FULFILMENT	Getting started takes effort – after just a few stretches, I feel energised and ready for the day.
6.45 am Showered	CONTENTED	Find the warmth of the shower is comforting. Great space for thinking and planning.
Now your go! – take one hour of your day and notice all the fluctuation in your feelings		

Caveat – I'm not a medical expert. Some conditions and medication can impact a person's level of awareness and emotional responses (e.g. depression, anxiety and medications that supress or increase neurochemicals, such as cortisol, adrenalin, serotonin and dopamine), so please be aware of this.

How was that? How many different feelings did you capture within your first two waking hours?

In only a couple of hours you will have experienced several shifts in feelings. More than you realise, probably. The ones you notice more are usually those where the situation has been a bit of a surprise, such as a news item that shocks you, or the rare time that your child gets up without you having to repeatedly chase them!

Feelings you are less aware of are those that come from an emotional trigger that is deemed as non-threatening or a low threat, and so doesn't require drastic action.

These emotional shifts can sometimes be seen by others: for example, a smile when you spot that the first flower of spring has bloomed. The feeling you attach to that could be hopefulness for warmer and lighter days. What about when you take a sip of your tea and its gone cold and you pull a face! This is an emotional response indicating displeasure. The feeling you attach to that could be annoyance.

Imagine how many feelings you're experiencing in one day. The people you lead will be experiencing as many as you, but they may be different, with different reasons for them.

If the shifts in feelings are like a rollercoaster lurching from feeling to feeling, this is where emotional management comes in, i.e. noticing, and acting appropriately to level yourself out.

What you are trying to do here is control your response, rather than react in an instant. Consider an airline pilot who has an engine failure. Their ability to stay calm allows them to tap into their knowledge and logically reason their way through a high-risk situation.

For example:

You have received a rather spiky email criticising a team member. You are inclined to respond immediately to such 'nit picking', as you see it, after all, the sender is not perfect.

Instead, though, you get up, take a deep breath and set off to make a cuppa. When you get back to your desk and re-read the email, your viewpoint is calmer. You pick up the phone to the team member to check out how they are finding working with this person (the sender). This pause both acknowledges the feelings *and* allows the neocortex to reconnect you with better judgement.

How you are feeling, can be linked to how you view the world on a particular day. If you go back to the Bottom-Up, Outside-In, Top-Down (bio-psycho-social) model, how you are feeling can be influenced by your biology, psychology, physiology *and* external factors (people, news etc). The more you acknowledge and manage these areas, the healthier you are and the calmer your brain can be.

TIP – Changing emotions – Four simple ways to manage emotions.

- Just **move** – you can stretch, walk around the room or march on the spot

- Through moving you can also **change the environment** - go outside, move to work in another room or at a different desk

- **Talk to someone** – you could check in with them about how you are feeling or find out about their day

- **Breathe**. The most accessible way to help calm emotions is with your breath. Box breathing is one to try.

Imagine four sides of a box:

- Side one, breathe in for four counts

- Side two, hold that breathe for four counts

- Side three, breathe out for four counts

- Side four, hold that breathe for four counts

Repeat side one and the whole cycle a few times.

You'll read later in this book about certainty, and how that helps calm the brain. Breathing in a box rhythm a few times calms the brain by re connecting it to the neo cortex. How? By focusing on the counting comfort is gained by the certainty of the pattern that box breathing provides. Steady breathing also provides a better supply of oxygen to aid body function and thinking.

Some or all of these activities only require a few minutes and will help you adjust your feelings to ones that will serve you better.

Describing feelings: in the feelings exercise above, how many additional 'feeling' words, to the ones listed, did you use?

One of the challenges in recognising and understanding emotions that I've come across over the years, is the limited use of emotional vocabulary and the difficulty people have in expressing their feelings accurately.

An example: Countless times I'm none the wiser when I ask after someone and they respond with phrases such as, 'All good', 'So so', 'Could be worse' or 'Don't ask!' How often do you reply similarly?

As a coach, and for you as leaders, this can limit how you respond. More information allows you to discover e.g. if they're deflecting, not knowing how to explain or not feeling able to say something. This then means that you can respond more appropriately.

When people do name their feelings, an understanding of their interpretation of that word is also important. For example:

'How are you?'

'Angry because 'x' said they'd cover for me at this meeting and they aren't in yet.'

When others hear you describe how you feel about something as e.g. 'angry' they will filter that word to fit in with their own understanding of it, and act (or not) on that.

This is where your emotional vocabulary comes into play. Angry might be the right word – or could another word for your feeling on the matter describe it better? Such as, peeved, irritated, or stronger still, livid? Allocating the most accurate label possible to your feelings is part of being able to manage your emotions. It helps you to identify how near or far you are from being calm (the space that allows for better cognitive judgement).

Can you see how, as a leader, your emotional interpretations (of yourself and others) relates directly to your response? This can then ripple through to other people (social awareness). Also, other people's reactions to *their* emotions and feelings can ripple through to you!

This is one way that an organisation's culture/s are created. 'Behaviour breeds behaviour.'

What is emotional intelligence (EQ)?

Emotional Intelligence is the *'ability to monitor one's own and other people's emotions, to discriminate between different emotions and label them appropriately, and to use emotional information to guide thinking and behaviour.'* (Salovey and Mayer 1990)

Daniel Goleman, who is arguable the best known in the area of EQ describes it as a combination of recognition and regulation: *'the ability to recognise, assess, control and utilise your own emotions and those of others.'*

- Recognition – self-awareness (of your own emotions) and social awareness (reading the room, listening to others, empathy)

- Regulation – self-management (regulating /responding appropriately) and relationship management (handling conflict, collaborating)

If you're not versed in the skill of recognising your emotions, and your feelings in response to them, and you aren't able to effectively manage those feelings, this could cause difficulties for you and could lead to an unhealthy (even toxic) environment for those you work with.

Poor EQ skills can negatively affect trust, performance and how well you build relationships across your world of work (and life). How? Because unmanaged emotions and emotional volatility can cause uncertainty, break or prevent trust, and even raise the level of fear in those around you.

GOOD NEWS: emotional awareness and management is a strength which can be developed with practice. This strength for managing emotions also plays a key role in increasing your resilience and level of courage.

Widening your emotional vocabulary is a great starting point for raising your EQ.

How do I know what I feel?

Clues to help you describe your state can be found by your motivation to act.

Let's say, something or someone has got your attention. Is you motivation to act high, medium or low? Is the driver for that motivation triggered by your perception of it as being something to withdraw from, or to be drawn to? Does it make you feel optimistic or more pessimistic?

Whether you're experiencing something you deem to be pleasant or unpleasant, if the intensity is high, e.g. joyful or livid, others will be more likely to notice it in your behaviour.

I put this image (Feelings Circle) together (see further on) to show how 'feeling' words can align to levels of emotional intensity.

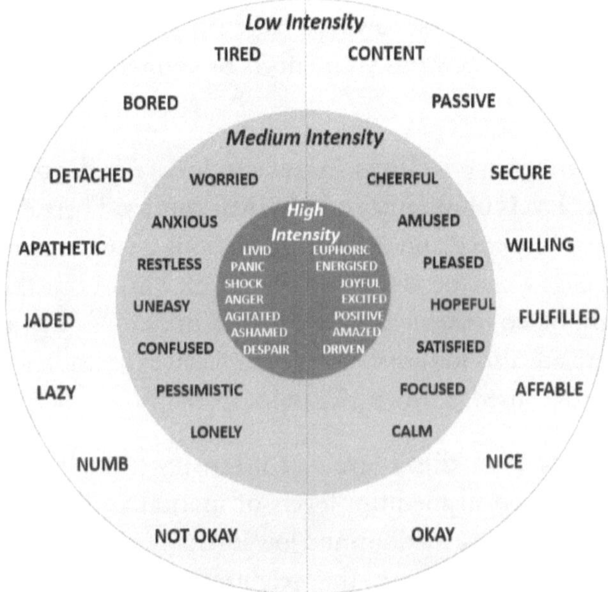

High intensity feelings (centre circle) result in high mental alertness and high levels of physical energy. Sustained periods of high intensity are draining and can lead to impulsivity and exhaustion. High intensity feelings can show up as fidgeting (you are itching to do or say something), talking over others (you can't wait), facial expressions and obvious changes in body language (which are unconscious and difficult to supress). Cheering, clapping and swearing are signs of feelings of high intensity.

As you can see, these behaviours can be linked to both pleasant and unpleasant feelings. When something important to you is impacted, a high intensity feeling will come with it, e.g. when a baby is born, you cut your finger, a dear person passes away, a large project gains you an award, someone steals your efforts or you receive a thank you.

Low intensity feelings (outer circle) are reflected in lower levels of mental and physical energy. There is less energy displayed and little or no obvious change in body language – maybe you physically shrink a little, but there might be no urgency to take part, ask questions or to act. There are also minimal changes to facial expression – an eyebrow raised, a frown or a smirk, perhaps.

Feelings of medium levels of intensity (middle circle) are reflected in medium levels of mental and physical energy. **Positive** medium and low intensity emotions help to optimise judgement, the weighing up a situation and decision making.

Aim to have 70% of your time in a medium to low level
intensity, positive, state
for your overall wellbeing and for clear thinking.

Please note: The intensity of feeling is an indication of an individual's alertness to a situation: low intensity is not always negative and high energy is not always positive, and vice versa. It's worth noting that sustained periods of low /negative feelings can lead to depression.

Other insights about feelings that can help you manage them:

- Feelings are information to be acknowledged

- Thoughts can generate feelings

- Feelings can generate thoughts

- Physiological reactions indicate strength of feeling

Idea: Knowing why you feel as you do can be hard to explain. The model below can stimulate greater clarity as to why you feel as you do. It can also be a starting point, to help those you lead understand their feelings and the personal needs that could be behind them.

For example, have you ever felt angry because a team member has gone home or is not contactable and a deadline has been missed. A need to respect your time could be what you see as not being met.

Perhaps you received some feedback on a conversation of more than six months ago, that revealed appreciation for a suggestion that had worked. You feel proud in that moment as your impact needs have shown to have been met.

Leaders I coach often have conflicting feelings, especially when they have to take on something new to them, which can be exciting and at the same time they procrastinate or delay decisions due to feelings of fear that have arisen with the need to step out of their comfort zone.

Feelings Table

Unpleasant Feelings e.g. Unmet Personal Needs	Conflicting Feelings e.g. Mixed Personal Needs	Pleasant Feelings e.g. Met Personal Needs
• **Anger** – Limits, fairness, respect • **Frustration** – Clarity, ability, advancement • **Fear** – Safety, stability, ease • **Loneliness** – Seen, understood, closeness • **Guilt** – Integrity, moral compass	• **Fear and Joy** – Safety, excitement • **Frustration and Love** – Ability, seen • **Loneliness and Pride** – Understood and impact • **Guilt and Appreciated** – Integrity and validation	• **Joy** – Connection, meaning, excitement • **Calm** – Safety, rest, certainty • **Love** – Belonging, closeness, seen • **Pride** – Progress, satisfaction, impact • **Appreciated** – self worth, validation, significance

To widen your emotional vocabulary even further, see the Hoffman Institute's comprehensive list of feeling words (see Sources and Further Reading). This not only suggests a multitude of feelings but also the bodily sensations that can appear alongside them.

Practise noticing sensations, the *intensity* of feeling related to a sensation, and then identify the most suitable 'feeling' word or words to describe the circumstances.

Here's how to increase emotional self-management.

When you can name what you're feeling with an idea of why you feel that way (your needs) you can think about how to manage it, i.e. either maintain it or change it, especially if it isn't helpful to you (or others), in relation to what you're doing or are about to do.

At the time of writing this chapter I chose to be *curious* and *engaged* so that my concentration levels were high, and I focused on what I wanted to achieve with the chapter.

Pick a feeling (from the Feeling Circle, or Hoffman list, for example) that will best serve you and what you seek to achieve in the next hour, and see what happens.

Ideas on how to manage your emotions. Having a desired feeling in mind helps to shift your feelings. Other suggestions to help establish a desired feeling are listed below. For the top suggestions on the list it may take just two minutes to start making the shift you seek. Nutrition, sleep and temperature changes can take longer to take effect and therefore warrant your ongoing care and attention.

- Movement – exercise, tidying, dancing

- Going outside, changing rooms, taking a break

- Listening to music – which makes you want to move, smile, relax

- Silence, quiet time, white noise

- Watching a movie that makes you laugh

- Social interactions – an act of kindness, people who energise or calm you, having a meet-up or asking for help

- Nutrition – having healthy foods and drinks

- Rest – getting regular sleep, reading

- Environment – adjusting the temperature, the location, facilities

Applying this to leadership

Imagine you've just heard that you've gained a vital qualification that will help your career and progression in the workplace. You're feeling ecstatic. Your next meeting is in two minutes, and you're about to give some feedback to a team member regarding some errors, highlighted by a key client.

- What would be the best way to feel, going into that meeting? Use the Feeling Circle image above or the Hoffman Institute Feelings List.

- What will you do to shift yourself toward your desired feeling?

- What can *you* do if your team member comes to the meeting with a high intensity energy (they could be feeling excited, agitated) or a low intensity energy (they could be feeling nervous, uninterested)?

You've been told that the targets for your team are going to get tougher, and you're worried about the impact of this. You tried to renegotiate them, but the targets have still been raised.

- How do you feel about the situation?

- What feeling (or feelings) would help you to share this message professionally, and in a way that enables the team to be able to open up with their perspectives and ideas?

Mood and health

I suggest that a goal for leaders includes your and your team's health and wellbeing as the expectations, work and responsibilities are addressed and implemented.

As the previous image indicates, bodily systems and minds work better and are healthier when you spend seventy percent of your time in feelings which are positive and of a low to medium intensity. Too long in unpleasant, high or low intensity ways of feeling are indicators of stress which can be harmful physically (due to the impact on the workings of your bodily systems) and mentally.

Spotting the development of a low mood in yourself or in a team member is a sign to make changes or ask for help.

What are you looking out for? Knowing yourself and your team well matters: it's part of your responsibility as a leader of others. The more in tune you are with the individuals in your team, the more noticeable it will be to you that their mood is 'different to normal'. Don't ignore such changes, privately say what you notice and ask if something has changed for them.

To conclude: Because everything is linked to emotions, feelings and moods, when leaders know how they feel they can choose to adjust that feeling, and therefore their behaviour. Leaders can also recognise when they feel vulnerable, overwhelmed or scared. *All* of your feelings are part of your authenticity.

By practising self-awareness, naming your feelings, and undertaking self-management you will also assist those around you to be in a healthier emotional state. This means managing your energy and openness so that you hear, understand and have empathy. This will help you to be a more effective and healthier leader.

TIP to influence a group's mood: At the start of a meeting you could ask, 'What can we agree is the best mindset and mood for us to hold during this meeting? What do we need to be doing to achieve that?'

Just asking the question can create a positive shift in people's feelings.

Reflection space

This is your space to note your ideas and actions as a result of reading and taking part in this chapter.

Chapter 4
Authenticity: understanding yourself with ongoing reflection

In my introduction I suggested that whatever your behaviour, actions or response to something or someone, you're being authentic, and you are. You just might not be being your *best* authentic self.

In Chapter 1 we looked at the story you tell yourself. How your memory plays a critical part in how you perceive things, indicating your values and beliefs.

In Chapter 2 we explored some neuroscience facts, such as how your mind will 'make things up', will predict and will seek to save energy through the development of habits. Some of which are not so useful, especially when you have leadership responsibilities.

In Chapter 3 we got emotional and discovered how central your emotions are to everything you do. How managing them comes with emotional awareness – knowing what you're feeling. This is to enable the possibility of shifting to a state that is more beneficial to you and others, i.e. having emotional intelligence.

Here in Chapter 4, we'll continue to explore your self-awareness (and your emotional intelligence), as a tool that informs whether you're being you most authentic self. We'll look more closely at your values, psychological safety, being vulnerable, beliefs and the reality of leading authentically – take your time, there is lots to reflect on.

To get going, ask yourself:

- Have you ever left a situation dissatisfied with how you conducted yourself within it?

- Have you ever 'gone with the group', even when you didn't want to, and knew it wasn't right or what you'd choose to do?

- On what occasions have you sat on the fence with your views, or stayed silent even when you knew which side you were on?

- If you're a leader at this time, how is your relationship with *your* manager impacting the way you lead and behave?

- When have you lied about, or embellished, a situation?

What does being your best, authentic self, mean? An explanation that I connect with, and hope you will, comes from Mike Shreeve (The No Pants Project).

'Be authentic by being honest with yourself and being open to how you aren't a perfect person.'

Your values are your guide

The work in this chapter draws on some reflection from the previous chapters, alongside honesty. In Chapter 1, reflection included: How is your story shaping your values and what matters to you? A large part of what makes you authentic are your core values. They work under the surface of us all and underpin your emotional responses, actions and judgements.

A value in action

A person sees someone struggling to get through a closed door. They are carrying a load of boxes and have their hands full. There are plenty of people around to help, but only one offers to and hold the door open. The door holder person is late, has a meeting to get to and a report to deliver, yet they interrupt their momentum to help.

Values are part of what is steering this decision to assist, even when they are under pressure themselves. Helping someone out mattered, and was important enough to them that they couldn't ignore it.

When you live, lead and act your values, your brain's reward system is triggered (dopamine, serotonin, oxytocin for example can be released). You feel good! Anticipation of that feeling creates a surge of dopamine, which motivates you to seek out opportunities to behave as per your values. Your values become part of your 'habit' system, as mentioned in Chapter 2: an unconscious way of being, thinking and feeling to navigate the world.

Your core values are...

You may well be clear on your values. Others, not so. Here is a chance to discover them or to check in with them.

From the words below, pick five (only five), that encapsulate what deeply matters to you. Values that you know impact how you live, lead and conduct yourself. Ways of being that you want from others, and that inform how you make choices and assessments.

If a word that describes your values is not shown, use it as one of your top five. This isn't an exhaustive list, more of a prompt. Again, pick only five (however hard that may be). More than five disguises what is most important to your way of being.

Adventure	Fitness	Joy/Play	Relationships
Affection	Forgiveness	Leadership	Respect
Balance	Freedom	Learning	Time
Beauty	Friendship	Love	Transparency
Career	Generosity	Loyalty	Speed
Caring/Kindness	Goodness	Meaning	Security
Change	Gratitude	Money	Self-worth
Connectivity	Happiness	Natural world	Sex
Collaboration	Health	Openness	Spirituality/Faith
Challenge	Honesty	Optimism	Strength
Creativity	Humour	Order	Success
Courage	Humanity	Patience	Teamwork
Diversity	Inclusion	Peace	Trust
Encouragement	Innovation	Perseverance	Wealth
Empathy	Integrity	Power	Well-being
Fairness	Intelligence	Precision	Wisdom
Family	Intuition/Gut	Recognition	Zen

My values are:

1.

2.

3.

4.

5.

Recognising your own values, gives you conscious awareness of how your thoughts and actions are coming about. Values play into your needs and as noted in Chapter 3, how you feel is impacted by those needs being met or otherwise.

A value in action

A coaching client told me about a team member who 'lives for the day'. They frequently said, *'I could be dead tomorrow' or 'You can't take it [money] with you.'* They were always, it seemed, on or booking leave for a trip somewhere, arranging or attending a party or treating friends. What made 'Adventure' (my interpretation of their value, it could be a different word for them) matter so much to them? There could be many reasons, although my coachee suspected it might be because they had lost a friend when they were a teenager and saw how our time on earth is limited. My coachee was envious of them to a point, although they did raise issues around this way of being, which highlighted their own values. They wondered at this team member's level of commitment to their role. That view is likely value based. The coachee having a set of values that may have included such things as reliability or dependability.

On capturing your values, you'll be able to notice that you speak in terms of your values; you'll see how you mostly act in line with them, and how you'll think and judge others by them.

Understanding the judgement part of your values is important, with regard to your leadership behaviour. Your values will differ from those you lead and need to influence, and you may not agree with someone else's values or they yours. In this case, an organisation's or team's values will serve you well as the over-arching guide and boundaries for acceptable workplace behaviour.

Like you, your team, clients and colleagues, along with friends and family, are all assessing each other based on their personal values. Guessing the reason behind someone's motives for using certain words, behaviour or actions can be clouded by your values system. The opportunity for you is to respectfully inquire into their reason for them.

Exploring the values you live and lead by a little more:

Explore each of your five values individually.

- What are the experiences and situations of your life that have given rise to each of your five values being so significant?

- Consider a recent decision at work or at home: which of your five values have been involved in that decision and how?

- **When** you've judged someone in a negative way, which of your values could *their* actions or behaviour be misaligning with yours? Have you been fair to them?

Values can give you courage. They can stimulate you to show the core of yourself, especially when you feel a need to defend yourself (your opinion or physically), others or a situation.

For example

I'd say (others may disagree) that I'm mostly mild mannered. However, that can change if I think you've been unnecessarily rude. Respectfulness is an important value to me. This came out when I was in a departure lounge, and someone was rude to airline crew when a flight was delayed in boarding. I stepped in to say that, however annoying and frustrating the situation was, being rude wasn't helping, and that it was unlikely that the boarding delay was a deliberate act by the departure gate team.

When I see people being respectful to each other, such as saying please and thank you, I gain pleasure from that.

On another occasion, I saw a team member throw some paper into a bin under their desk, only it missed. I pointed out that it had missed, and the response was that the cleaners would clear it up. *'No,'* I said, *'you will, the cleaner empties the bins, it's not their responsibility to fill them!'*

There have been times when I haven't been true to my values and when I haven't said what I wanted. Like the 'to get going' questions at the start of this chapter, there have been times when I've hidden the person I really am. Why was this? Because sometimes I didn't interpret the environment as 'safe enough' to do so.

Safe spaces - Leaders who help others to feel 'safe enough' provide their people with an environment in which to live their values.

When you or others don't feel 'safe enough', actions and behaviour can become supressed or 'out of character'. What enables 'safe enough'? You may recall how in a previous chapter I advised that the brain's role is to keep you safe, to aid a long and productive life, and that being part of groups and being valued by others is an inherent way for humans to gain a sense of safety. An article by Edmondson and Mortensen (2023) in the Harvard Business Review describes 'safe enough' (also known as psychological safety), as *the belief that one can speak up without risk of punishment or humiliation'.*

That sense of 'safe enough' is not constant, it can vary, moment by moment, for a leader as much as for their team and the others they work with. Did you spot the reflection question at the start of this chapter - when have you lied about or embellished a situation? In this case, if this applies to you, what was your reason? It could have been to do with a value you hadn't met.

For example:

You have a value for efficiency, yet you've struggled to complete a task or deal with a situation. You lie to cover it up or delay others realising this. Your sense of self is at risk. You haven't been able to meet your own standard and, more importantly, you haven't felt able to accept that and be honest with others about it.

As a leader you can create 'safe spaces' for your team. Consider the quote from earlier:

'Be authentic by being honest with yourself and being open to how you aren't a perfect person'.

Your ability, as a leader and a business owner, to share your vulnerabilities, will go a long way towards creating an atmosphere of trust that can give your team and colleagues the confidence to share their thoughts, ideas and criticisms. This means tapping into and expressing your feelings in a professional manner and using your values to communicate.

Example – Using your values to lead authentically and with empathy

One senior leader I coached (I'll call them John) did the values exercise which revealed his values to be: Cooperation, Fairness, Integrity, Trust and Competence. John was having to implement a performance management process with a team that he'd only recently inherited, and who hadn't been given objectives or had performance reviews for a few years. He didn't know them well yet and was concerned about pushback and cynicism from a team he was still trying to connect to. In coaching we worked on how John could use his values (now that he was able to name them) to communicate 'why' this process mattered and 'what' it will enable for the team and their organisation.

With this new understanding of his values, John felt he could now authentically position the process, and uphold it, if and when pushback was received. We also thought about how others may feel vulnerable about performance reviews, so he put in place an approach that included space for one-to-one time and team time to hear any concerns.

These spaces would take time to feel 'safe enough' for everyone and so, referencing the quote, *'Be authentic by being honest with yourself and being open to how you aren't a perfect person'*, we dug deeper into John's own vulnerabilities in the performance management process, when he first experienced it as a team member and as a leader. This, he found, would be useful to reference as a genuine way to connect with his team's concerns.

Values and vulnerability

Change, such as the introduction of a new system, is psychologically challenging to varying extents for each of us: our brain often seeks consistency and will create resistant behaviour when faced with having to do things differently. Change is one example, but other situations can also cause feelings of vulnerability, such as when a leader has a poor performer in their team.

The leader, the performer and their teammates may all feel degrees of vulnerability about this matter and its implications for them personally. If that vulnerability is allowed to flourish, it can result in someone behaving outside of their own values (such as not saying what they think, not collaborating or losing their temper and being rude). When this occurs, there isn't dopamine, rather, stress is increased (the neurochemical cortisol* is released) and, generally, people don't feel good about their actions or non-actions.

*Stress is important for motivation and galvanising our focus too – Cortisol is an essential neurochemical, not a 'bad' one (unless it's constant), as I hear it describe at times.

Questions on values and vulnerability

- Being honest, when do you as a leader or business owner feel vulnerable? In what situations or with which people?

- How are you likely to behave at such times that don't align with your values?

- What is the result of that behaviour for you and those affected?

Earlier, I said that **values can make you brave, but not always**

- Consider how, as the imperfect person we all are, you could (find the courage to) get to a solution to overcoming your barriers

- What one small step could move you closer to acting from your values (and more authentically) when faced with your area of vulnerability in the future?

- What difference would that small step make to your reputation as a leader or a business owner, to the situation of concern and any others involved?

Beliefs – have you some that prevent you from being the leader you seek to be?

Your beliefs: are they helping or hindering you living your values? Let's explore the role of beliefs.

Beliefs according to the Oxford English Dictionary are:

1. An acceptance that something exists or is true,

especially one without proof

2. Trust, faith or confidence in someone (including yourself) or something

An article by psychologist Daniela Kirova (2023), on the Values Institute website relates to the studies of Carl Rogers about the identity of self. How you see yourself is presented in how you tell the story of your life (an earlier chapter) and your experiences. These stories, as you relate them, reveal your self-image. This could include both positive and negative beliefs. How you see yourself connects to your level of self-esteem and your self-image, which can be different to how others see you!

I've seen this using 360-degree feedback (feedback from multiple sources), when coaching leaders. How you score yourself on a statement such as 'communicates clearly', is an indicator of your self-image that can be compared with how others rate you. If you score yourself low or high, and others rate you differently, this provides rich insight to explore around your self-image, and the experience of the respondents in your feedback.

The opportunity, therefore, can be to explore your beliefs about yourself and possibly adjust them.

Example

One of my clients knew their stuff, yet when it came to demonstrating their expertise with their manager, and in meetings, they held back even though they wanted to put a view across or pose a question. We talked about their reasons for this, and the person revealed that they anticipated and dreaded the possibility of their view being challenged. Further exploration into how conflict had played out in their life revealed that, in their younger years, they'd regularly been put down by a parent, if they'd questioned the parent or raised an idea. This had developed into a belief that others, especially authority figures, knew more or better than them, and that it was therefore 'safer' to keep quiet to avoid disapproval or humiliation.

Our reflection in coaching allowed the person to check if this belief, 'that questioning others' views can lead to conflict and humiliation' was actually true. The coachee decided it wasn't and went away with a changed view of themselves. That shift and the confidence it gave them, enabling them to speak up, aligned them to their values and they displayed a more authentic self as a result. This also positively impacted how others saw them.

Beliefs (and values) form your identity

Reflection and being coached in identifying your values and beliefs requires vulnerability and honesty. If in reflecting, you realise that your former beliefs e.g. 'What I want isn't important', 'I'm not as competent as...', 'If only I'd achieved "x", life would be so much better', 'If I speak up no one will listen' or 'I'm stupid', are not true, then the opportunity to reset them is invaluable to you and to your identity as a leader.

Conversely, your belief could be that 'you are the best', 'perfection is paramount', 'you are the only one who can do "x"', and so on. I've had leaders work with me who reveal how they judge others as weak or less than them and so might discount engaging with those individuals. The reflection opportunity here is to pinpoint how this belief came about. Then to assess how often this belief is actually true.

It takes focused reflection, and the building of empathy for self and others, to address beliefs. I find that, generally, people can be self-critical and tough on themselves, and frustrated that they are, like everyone else, flawed and a work in progress.

The more you work on understanding yourself, however uncomfortable it can be (those emotions again), the more opportunities you'll discover to progress your sense of self. That progress will better align you to your values and how you live them, such as standing up for what you believe in!

Question to consider around your beliefs as a leader

- What kind of leader do you want to be?

- How do you want others to describe you as a

leader?

- What beliefs would that leader have?

- How are your beliefs aligned to the kind of leader you want to be (your answer to the first question)?

- If they are some differences, what impact is that having on your leadership identity?

- Which of your beliefs prevent you from being the leader you desire to represent?

Beliefs, like values, can make you brave. They can motivate you and give you energy, so, for example, encourage you to speak up. However, that's not always the case. Your beliefs about yourself can prevent you from having the courage to be the leader you really want to be.

The cost of your authenticity in leadership and life

Earlier I stated that authenticity, being guided to follow your values and beliefs, can require courage. Being authentic comes with challenges and sacrifices. Authenticity requires a strong sense of self and the ability for self-validation, when your stance may not be popular.

Authenticity as a leader requires you to put your head above the parapet, to stand out. This gives others the opportunity to act in ways that impact on your innate survival psychology to feel valued and included. You may not always feel 'safe enough'.

Responses to your way of leading (even when they come from your values) can lead to criticism, rejection and even ridicule from others who feel threatened by your perspective, or just disagree with it.

Authenticity – you as your best self, means that as a leader you take responsibility for your decisions or mistakes, often publicly. Which is one of the reasons why leaders can find leadership a lonely place, especially if they're not able to develop allies they can open up too.

If you're a leader who wishes to inspire others to be authentic, to be open and courageous, one of your goals can be to role-model that way of being, consistently.

In summary

You're being authentic in how you respond in any moment because an emotion, a belief, a memory, a prediction and your values are interplaying. It's when you're not aware of what those contributing factors are that you can limit your own potential.

Leaders who do the work of regular self-reflection and gathering knowledge of themselves, increase their self-worth and gain a sense of safety that allows them to show up in their most authentic way.

As the quote at the beginning says – I know, I keep repeating it...

'Be authentic by being honest with yourself and being open to how you aren't a perfect person.'

Leaders who feel safe, help others to feel safe enough to explore who they are too. People join groups, teams and businesses and stay in them when they feel safe. The benefit to team performance comes through spaces that allow teams to be curious, to innovate, to fail and to learn in a supportive environment.

As leaders are part of the culture-creation of a business they, in my view, have a responsibility for the culture they're creating. I think we all know leaders who feed a culture of fear and dread. You, though, have the ability, even in a small way, to create a positive culture through your authenticity to be the best leader you can.

The questions and reflections in this chapter are something you can learn from and revisit many times. Add any thoughts and ideas in this reflection space below.

A reflection question and place for your notes: What can I do as a leader, business owner or person of influence to create spaces that are safe enough for those I meet or work with to be authentic?

Chapter 5

Knowing Others: keeping your relationship bank account in credit

So far, this book has focused on you understanding yourself and on giving you the space to review and update who you are. As you progress through this book, further insights will continue to enable this growth and provide ideas for you to practise and try out as a leader. The aim is that you lead as the person you know yourself to be, as often and as fully as possible.

There is a good reason for this, because regret comes from not 'being' that person. If you think back to the previous chapter, and the reflection question around a time when you lied, embellished, overreacted or stayed silent, often such a situation results in feelings of regret or of having let yourself down.

Knowing yourself and having the confidence to be yourself, in terms of the previous chapters, means that you can increasingly reveal the best of yourself as a leader, business owner or someone who trades on trust, such as a solicitor, client manager or financial advisor.

Self-knowledge is gold dust for many reasons, one of which is in relationship building. Leadership positions of all kinds, by their nature, involve connecting with other people. When I've asked groups and teams, *'What will make this session successful?'* of the many words that come out trust is always on the list. But what does 'trust' actually mean and how does it apply in terms of what you as a leader say or do? And what impact does what you say or do have on those you lead and influence?

Example - Trustworthiness can seem intangible, but this model from David Maister, Robert Galford and Charlie Green, authors of *The Trusted Advisor,* helps break it down into an equation.

$$T = \frac{C + R + I}{S}$$

Trustworthiness = your **credibility** + your **reliability** + **intimacy** levels

and how much **self-orientation you have**

To gain trustworthiness, this model suggests that you should aim to score highly with those you influence in the following three areas:

Credibility: the trust others have in what you say – your expertise, knowledge and insights.

Reliability: the level of trust you generate by your actions – you do what you say you will and are dependable.

Intimacy: how safe people are with you – you are approachable, you keep confidences, and you don't belittle or embarrass.

Reduced or broken trustworthiness: according to the model, this comes about when you have been strongly focused on yourself.

Self-orientation: a high score here indicates self-interest, concern for what *you alone* get out of something and that you don't appear to care as much about others. However, it's worth noting that a leader may be thinking of themselves *and* their team, which would lower this score.

Three questions - A trustworthiness audit

Question 1 – Considering your role's demands and expectations, **list who you need to make and maintain strong relationships with.** Notice that I said: make *and* maintain. Create an extensive list of names. These headings may assist you to identify people:

- Customers and clients

- Direct reports – your team

- Peers and colleagues

- Senior management and executives

- Board members

- Suppliers

- Community leaders and influencers

- Regulators and government officials

- Shareholders and investors

- Industry associations and professional networks

Each of these groups has unique needs and expectations, and ways in which they will perceive your trustworthiness. Ensuring that you engage with them relevantly and regularly, understand their concerns, and work collaboratively, can significantly enhance your relationships and leadership effectiveness.

Question 2 – In what ways are you showing these different individuals and groups that you are trustworthy? This template can be used to capture your trustworthiness audit details.

Name/ Relationship					
Ways I show credibility					
Ways I show reliability					
Ways I show intimacy					
Ways I show they matter					
Actions points. Do more or less of...					

The value of relationship credits

The idea with the trust equation is to be conscious of your actions and behaviour, so you have awareness of where and when, as a leader, you have credits or debits in your important relationships.

We all mess up sometimes (e.g. late with a report, missing a critical detail, omitting to attend a key meeting) and your track record builds credits that will provide some grace for an occasional mistake. How you respond to your mistakes will help refill or empty your credits to

Example

Building **credit**: a leader I worked with described how she had joined a new company and became the leader of the business development team. On arrival it became clear that the team were sceptical of her. She asked her manager about the situation and learnt that the previous leader had left without warning and hadn't done what he'd said he'd do. The team had trusted him but had been let down, not just in the work that they'd had to pick up, but also personally, as he'd been likeable and seemed to have connected with them.

On learning this, the new leader held a team meeting. She shared what she'd learnt and expressed how sorry she was that they'd had to experience that. She showed them the trust equation and suggested that they make a charter for how they would work together.

She went on to say that they could call her out, and that they could call each other out if anyone fell short of what their charter agreed (see Chapter 8 for ideas for co-creating a charter with your team). From the charter, which included some quality standards, she pulled out the team's values and used these as a guide to how they would behave, alongside the other elements of the charter. She obtained these values from exploring with the team 'what we want to be recognised for.' This meeting set them all up well, and from there they could assess her and each other's credibility, reliability and intimacy, *and* call out high levels of self-orientation.

What can you do if there is a trust issue in the team?

Example

I'd been doing some team development with a senior team. They were spread around, globally, and after I'd had one-to-one conversations about the experience of being in the team, it was clear that levels of trust were uneven. One person created more frustrations than others within the group. No one doubted this person's skills and knowledge – their credibility. But their reliability fluctuated and seemed to be dependent on their interest in the work to be done (self-orientation). This person had ignored feedback on their behaviour (speaking to others dismissively, talking over them, etc.), when it was given by a colleague who was a new member of the senior team (intimacy). This peer, having tried to deal with the situation directly, sought assistance from the Managing Director (MD) as the behaviour continued. The trustworthiness of the MD gained credit because of the way they'd behaved when called upon for support. The MD started to notice the behaviour during online calls and reiterated behavioural expectations both in meetings and in general. The situation then improved somewhat.

But it turned out (through one-to-one conversations with the MD), that the person in question was no longer enthused by how they were required to do their role. Their interest was in the work itself, not in the team and the global corporate interactions that were now expected. The person left voluntarily a few months later, possibly because their values and beliefs were no longer a good match with the organisation's.

Being based in, or from, a different global location can lead to the intimacy element of the trust equation being neglected, or not given sufficient time and attention. Though being in the same location doesn't always mean that this element is given adequate focus either!

Next, see some ways to deal with this.

Knowing them – increasing intimacy

Earlier I used the phrase 'maintain' in terms of relationships. Taking time to get to know and appreciate a new team or team member is often a conscious practice. Maintaining and building that relationship will happen as this practice continues.

Here are a few ideas for increasing the 'intimacy' factor that you can try out as a leader, and encourage your team to adopt also:

- Making extra time ahead of and at the end of a meeting. Being early to a meeting (in-person or virtual) and having time to find out how other people's days are going, asking about their holidays and how their children's exams went, shows that you are interested in them, approachable and open to connecting more personally. You can also consider staying back at the end of a meeting to do the same

- Arranging to have lunch or a tea break. I find that

most meetings between leaders or managers and their clients, or members of their team (including one-to-ones), are about 'the work'. By having regular catch ups that are non-work related, an opportunity is created to talk about more. 'Regular' might mean a quarterly team gathering (again virtual or in-person) and for one-to-ones, every couple of months. You can have a bit of fun with icebreakers or unusual venues – there are many online resources with ideas to suit any team. For example: BusinessBalls for Icebreaker Games

- Walking meetings. These can also be done virtually with two people, both parties using headphones (no need for cameras) and getting outside for meetings. A part of that meeting is a few moments about what's happening around both parties and this helps them to learn more about what it's like where the other person is. In-person walking meetings, either in pairs or as a team/group, create opportunities for mixing up a group. The change of environment shifts perspectives and opens up ideas and thoughts

- Encourage sharing, with you sharing some of your vulnerabilities as well, e.g. what you've found hard and how you overcame that. 'Lunch & learns' are often popular. If someone has an idea that could work for you and others too, thank them!

- Create rituals that encourage personal

connection – start meetings with a regular question, e.g. what made you smile this week?

- Pair people up for projects and rotate pairings and interactions where practically possible

For **even more ideas** see the Forbes reference (16 Effective Ways to Encourage Strong Team Relationships) in Sources and Further Reading.

Building relationships and maintaining them may not be something that comes naturally to you or to those you deal with. I've learnt, as have my clients, that your values and beliefs are a vital guide to many of the things you'll need to do as a leader. Applying them to how you build your relationships will allow you to be authentic in your approach, even if it feels awkward initially.

Example – Let's revisit the example of John in Chapter 4. His values were: Cooperation, Fairness, Integrity, Trust and Competence. For him to be able to show his team fairness, integrity and trust, he needed to know them individually and as a collective – to understand what they enjoyed and dreaded in their work, while also gaining insight into other factors that might impact how he worked with them and they with others. With his values as the headings to guide him in getting to know his team, John felt he could be genuine in his approach. He wasn't much for icebreakers himself, but he learnt through his conversations with the team (about past team events that had gone well) that they'd included some fun activities. Because it mattered to them, he suggested that monthly meetings start with an icebreaker, and that they take it in turns to choose one. Taking turns would reveal much about the person who chose a particular activity, therefore growing every team member's insight into the others and increasing intimacy for all.

There's a key skill to relationship building, and that's the art of listening. See below for a model of levels of listening. Note that the mood you're in will affect the level of listening you're using at any one time. For a fuller reminder, see Chapter 3 on emotions, where understanding how you feel, and adjusting it if required to something more suitable for the situation and outcome, are explained.

This listening/mindset model by MIT lecturer Otto Scharmer is one that I use in many situations. Listening is as essential for coaches as it is for leaders, managers and business owners. It helps prepare for difficult conversations and it can be a problem-solving aid for yourself with others, or in a group. It helps you to get to spaces of creativity and transformation. It's also useful to know when you find yourself listening at a superficial level.

The model below can help you to spot someone else's listening level and ask about it, e.g. 'You seem distracted. Is there something else on your mind?'

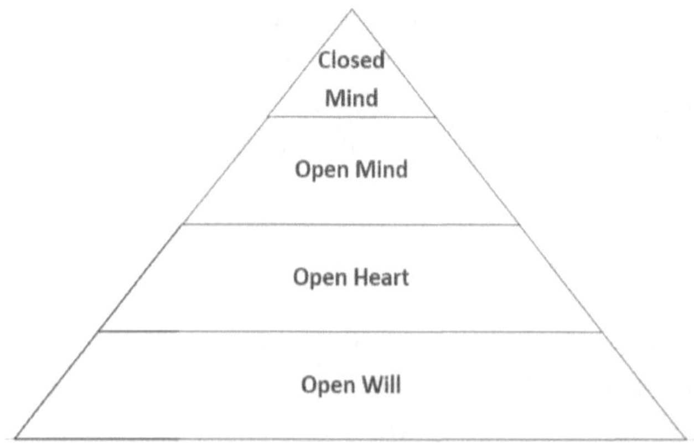

Below are some more details as to what the levels mean:

Closed Mind – When you know or think you know what's being said or inferred (that brain of yours is predicting again!). There's a low level of (or no) interest in engaging with the speaker at that time. Not only that, but you also have your view and that's that!

Open Mind – When you're taking notice of new knowledge and perspectives. What's being said is interesting to know and gets you thinking. But at this level you're not likely to change your mind about a decision, or your perspective on something.

Open Heart – Now you're feeling it! You're connecting to what's being heard and even who's saying it. It's more than information and facts. You empathise, and this enhances connection and mutual understanding. You're listening and connecting, which sparks consideration of your position or actions.

Open Will – With this mindset, you're connecting to the bigger potential of a conversation, to a greater purpose than your own desires or outcomes. You may well change your mind or shift your perspective about something or someone, because something more important can be achieved, even if you have to put aside some of your original preferences or feelings.

In certain situations, Open Mind would be better to apply at the outset than Open Will. For example, where certain rules must be adhered to, such as legalities, compliance rules or terms of agreement.

A case study: this example is based on a real situation. Amongst other things, it demonstrates the (significant) difference in impact a leader has based on their level of listening i.e. where their focus is (on themselves or on others). This links back to the trust equation and how they are managing their emotional state to enable their best handling of a situation.

As you read this case study, consider what levels of listening are being shown by the people mentioned below.

Jake (not his real name) had been working at a small but successful tech support firm for four years. He could be classed as a middle manager with a small team, and was doing well. His director, though busy, checked in regularly with Jake and was impressed with his progress. Jake found her easy to share ideas and concerns with and she gave Jake positive performance reviews with constructive and clear areas for improvement. Jake felt trusted because of the greater responsibilities he was given. He enjoyed going to work even when he felt challenged by some of the activities and timelines and having to steer his small team.

However, times change, and a restructure and a merger with a bigger organisation meant Jake had to report to a new director. It wasn't a problem, nothing to worry about. Jake's job was safe and he saw greater opportunities could be possible.

Until, after what seemed to be a good start, his new leader started to change. He wasn't just occasionally blunt and curt to the point of near rudeness. Having initially been amenable and shown appreciation of Jake's track record, in time this was no longer the case. Sighing loudly, raising his eyes to the ceiling when questioned and stomping around had become the norm. When Jake needed advice about the work he was to do, the new director was short and impatient with him.

One day, bothered by the change, Jake asked him if he was okay. The director replied that he was under pressure and didn't mean to cause upset. But a subsequent improved manner, lasted just one day. Jake kept trying to do his best but felt undermined and unsupported while at the same time micromanaged, as every little error was noted. He no longer wanted to come to work. Nevertheless, he decided to try one more time. When they were alone in the office, he asked the director if work pressures had changed, and if he could help. The director said no.

'What would help? Jake asked.

'Not being asked such personal questions,' the director replied.

The next day Jake went to HR. He was now miserable at work and it was affecting his home life. He also began to search for a new role.

There is much that can be unpicked from this example. Such as, what was causing the director so much stress? What did that person need, to help ease that? And did they feel able to ask for what they needed?

Listening to yourself and connecting to how you are behaving, will serve you well in being able to make suitable adjustments to enhance how you listen and lead. The SCARF model referred to Chapter 6 can also help this.

Take a moment to reflect on your listening levels over the last week. When has each of the levels been in play (you can't expect to be at Open Will level all of the time) and how was that particular level beneficial to your relationship with the speaker, and to the topic being discussed?

Listening Level	Situation	Might a different level have been better? If so, which one and why?
Closed Mind		
Open Mind		
Open Heart		
Open Will		

Relationships take work and as a leader your relationship skills can make or break the trust others have in you. If you find trust breaking down, the next chapter on courage and mental toughness will be very useful.

Reflection space

This is your space to note your ideas and actions as a result of reading and taking part in this chapter.

Chapter 6
Developing Mental Toughness

Mental Toughness vs Resilience

Mental toughness and resilience are often used interchangeably. As a leader it's unlikely that you'll avoid times of discomfort, pressure and personal challenge. Being a leader comes with expectations that you'll be able to handle these occasions. How do you navigate such situations professionally, consistently and authentically? And, how mentally tough do you think you need to be?

I now want to describe what mental toughness is and how it differs from, although it's closely linked to, resilience. My comments are based on the work of Clough, Strycharczyk and Perry who are lead researchers in the field of mental toughness – see the Sources section for further reading.

Their research found and comments that, *'Mental toughness is a personality trait which determines, in some part, how individuals perform when exposed to stressors, pressure, opportunity and challenge.'* (Clough, Strycharczyk and Perry, 2021).

Their research findings defined the elements of mental toughness as being 4Cs:

Control, Commitment, Challenge and Confidence, each C having two further parts (as shown in the adapted 4Cs diagram below):

Clough and others also describe how mental toughness levels are on a continuum from being more sensitive to being tougher.

As a personality trait, your level of mental toughness is pretty fixed. It can be assessed with the MTQPlus Assessment by AQR International, of which I am a practitioner, should you be interested.

My leadership coaching around mental toughness investigates your preferred behaviours (the report gives this clarity) and explores adaptations that can support better outcomes. The idea is to learn and practise adjustments so, for example, if you want a better impact in certain situations but maybe lack the self-belief to step in, *or* you create discord in the way you put across your ideas. Recognising this is the first step – the next is to make behaviour changes that fit with who you are authentically *and* enhance your leadership position.

An individual's level of optimism plays a key part in their mental toughness, for example, their attitude toward challenges, problem solving and overcoming difficulties. Resilience, i.e. keeping going and digging deep, is about withstanding, surviving and recovering from difficulties. Being mentally tougher means perceiving issues with a more positive lens, giving you the drive to get through barriers, while seeing the brighter side (and perhaps even exciting opportunities).

Mental toughness therefore is a combination of resilience *and* positivity. Mentally tough individuals are often resilient. Resilient individuals are not always mentally tough.

An example: My own mental toughness scores are middle of the road. This was a bit frustrating when I first got my MTQPlus results. I thought that I must be high in mental toughness, as I'd overcome many obstacles, such as when a ten-year-old business collapsed. Pushing through that challenge included getting work, finding a new home, rebuilding my finances, and facing feelings of shame and guilt. I created a career, gained experience and lots of qualifications. But, as my MTQPlus assessment report highlighted, it all took immense effort, I felt that I *had* to do this to survive. And, as you saw in the My Story chapter, it took me ten years to share this part of my life openly. I 'bounced back' eventually and had definitely been resilient, but optimism had often been lacking. I had times of deep dread and fear. Thankfully, that lowness of spirit, when facing difficulties, doesn't last as long now due to the learning I've acquired from my experiences. With the emotion tools mentioned earlier and the other ideas in this book, I can get to an optimistic perspective more quickly. I've developed and can behave in a more mentally tough way.

In this chapter you get to explore the 4Cs framework in more detail, as well as looking at a second concept (the SCARF Model). These tools can help you to analyse your behaviour, thoughts and feelings to identify the ways in which you could develop.

It's also worth noting that understanding mental toughness isn't to make everyone mentally tough, it's more about understanding your behaviour in a given situation and what's influencing it. It also enables you as a leader to better understand other people's behaviour.

A question for you – keep note of the answers

1. What aspects of your role as a leader or business owner put you under pressure or create anxiety, rather than being seen as an opportunity?

2. When such a situation occurs what is your response?

Becoming Mentally Tough – an example

Before I go on, if you go back to Chapter 2, where some neuroscience basics were highlighted, you'll recall how habits are formed by repetition, as the way your brain has for saving energy and keeping you safe. The information below explains this more, with an example of how courage and mental toughness in leadership can be developed with habit change and repetition.

The brain reward/habit system. If your habits cause you to shy away from certain leadership tasks or to go in too strongly, it's partly because of personality: that you've practised and learnt that 'this way is safe for me'. Because of that sense of safety and comfort, you repeat that way of being.

The idea for building mental toughness (positivity and resilience), is that you start to consciously check your default behaviour and see if another way is better. You then test that and, if it works, you repeat it and soon you've created another neural pathway as an alternative to the older one. The more you repeat the new behaviour the more natural it becomes.

Example: In the past, I used to dread having to say 'No'. I perceived that this might jeopardise a relationship and possibly invite conflict. The idea of being shouted at or having views dismissed in private or in public sent shivers through me. I knew that I'd then feel anxious for days afterwards. So, my brain generated the habit of saying 'Yes' as a way to protect me and 'keep me safe' (this is the brain's main job and is based on an innate drive for belonging, to ensure a greater chance of survival).

I knew that this wasn't always the best option and that as a leader (and in other life situations) always saying yes was no longer a good strategy. It also didn't sit well with my values and prevented me from acting with more authenticity, so I had to gain the courage to say 'No' when appropriate.

As a new manager, I felt brave the first time I said no. A team member wanted an advance payment of their wages. It wasn't the first time; in fact, it was the third time they'd asked. I felt bad for them and the situation they were in, but continuing to say yes was not going to help them in the long term or set a good precedent for others.

I said that I could no longer do this; that I was sorry they were having difficulties and reminded them of the employee assistance programme and the financial advice service it provided. The person was angry and, I think, scared. We talked for a while and I set them up with the call to get financial advice in a private office. A few weeks later, they shared how helpful that had been.

Habits form based on perceived safety needs and repetition. My example above shows how habits can be formed, reinforced and also reformed. The following diagram and example (as above) show what's happening subconsciously.

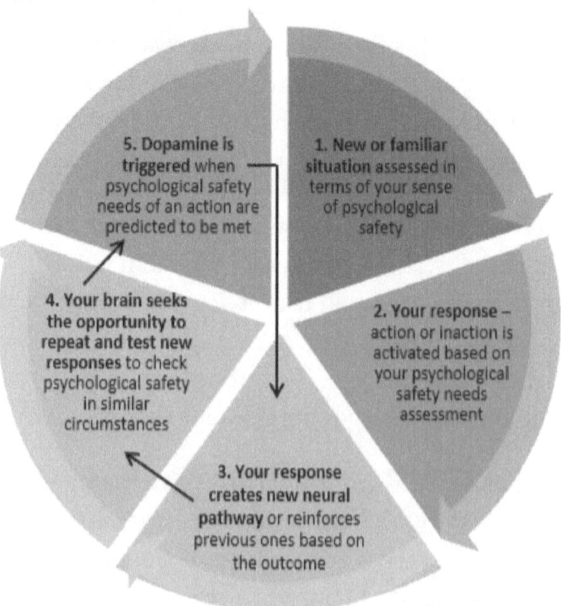

1. **A new or familiar situation**. So, for example, a team member asks for an advance of their wages. Previously, I'd said 'Yes'.

2. **Your response**. This time, instead of saying yes, I stepped into discomfort, challenged my previous habit and said '*No*' to the request.

3. **Your different response creates a new neural pathway.** The result was that the no didn't ruin the relationship, it changed it.

4. **Your brain seeks to repeat the new behaviour.** Emboldened, by the positive result of saying

no this time, new opportunities to say 'No' (where appropriate) were identified, practised and rewarded with dopamine, especially as the fears regarding saying no weren't realised.

5. **Dopamine**. This neurochemical is the reward for habit use and, in this example, the new habit pathway was strengthened the more it was used.

The arrows between steps 3 and 5 show how dopamine encourages repetition through anticipation of something that is deemed desirable, in terms of perceived safety needs or improvement.

Outcome – My mental toughness levels – the ability to perform well in real or perceived stressful situations had been tested. This example of a personally challenging situation (you will have different ones) gave me the opportunity to update my well-formed dread of saying no to this type of request. Altering my behaviour increased my confidence in facing similar situations again.

The secret is to test, learn and adapt, and to keep increasing your resilience and positivity in difficult situations with a wider range of habit options.

Concept 1 – Understanding what can be developed in terms of the 4Cs to improve how you lead during real and perceived difficult circumstances.

Look at each aspect of the 4Cs and its associated statement (which describes being mentally tough) below. Consider the question and challenge/s you noted down earlier in terms of these statements, and view how closely your attitude and behaviours match them.

Control – the level of control you think you have over life situations and your ability to recognise and manage your emotions when under pressure

- **I really believe I can do this**

- **I keep my emotions in check when doing this**

Commitment – your propensity to set goals, the number of goals, their difficulty, and your determination to achieve them

- I **promise to do it – I'll set a goal**

- I**'ll do what it takes to deliver the goal (hard work)**

Challenge – how comfortable you are with risk and your attitude to learning from errors and/or failings

- **I'm driven to do this – I will take a chance**

- **Setbacks make me stronger**

Confidence – how confident you feel in your own abilities, and your confidence in speaking up, challenging others and being challenged

- **I believe I have the ability to do this**

- **I can stand my ground if I need to**

With your challenge in mind:

- **Where** can you agree with the two statements for each of the 4Cs (above)?

- **If you** agree with a statement, how do you know it to be true? What evidence are you using?

- **If you** can't agree with a statement, or only somewhat, how do you know it to be true in this case? What evidence are you using?

- **Which** of the 4Cs require your attention? If you rate yourself highly in any/all areas, how might you adapt your behaviour to create an enhanced environment for others involved?

- **Who** do you know who is good at this part of your role (either the implementation or conducting themselves in a way that you think could be better for you and for others)?

As mentioned earlier, Clough and others promote the understanding that levels of mental toughness are on a continuum from being more sensitive to being tougher. That knowledge can help to explain behaviours and spot opportunities to adjust them.

Clough and others' research also looks at the pluses and minus at both ends of the mental toughness continuum. Such as:

- Mental toughness does not necessarily equate with great leadership behaviour

- Mental sensitivity does not necessarily equate with poor leadership behaviour

- The two are indicators of attitude and the level of energy and support that can be required to push through (this can apply to either the leader or the team member):

    - People (leaders or their team members) who are sensitive, can at times require more energy and support networks to achieve a result

    - People (leaders or their team members) who are tough can have a natural drive, focus and optimism and at times may need less in the way of support networks

- Too tough, too often – this kind of behaviour from a leader can appear inhumane, unemotional, over-committed, overstretched, reckless, not willing to learn from mistakes or overconfident in their abilities and themselves. Too tough, too often can burn a leader out and create anxiety in others who are more sensitive

- High sensitivity, too often (in a leader) can appear

rudderless, emotionally draining, hesitant to commit, slow-paced, overly cautious, pessimistic and self-doubting. High sensitivity, too often can increase anxiety in the leader themselves and in others

Leaders I have worked with have found that being able to understand their behaviour in response to their natural levels of mental toughness is beneficial for their performance and wellbeing.

As a leader, it's also helpful in terms of how you motivate others to achieve greater performance and for the person's wellbeing. As stated earlier, the idea of understanding mental toughness isn't to make everyone mentally tough, it's more about understanding behaviours and what is influencing them, and so acting appropriately.

Concept 2 – Have you ever had a 'feeling' about a situation that's bothering you?

Perhaps you feel 'out of sorts' about the situation. Maybe it's a person you have to say '*no*' to or how a situation is being handled? You go through the scenario in your mind, maybe you have physical sensations, or you get irritable with people who have nothing to do with it. When this has happened to me, it's been because I haven't been able to pinpoint what was getting to me.

This next concept helps to identify this, and so enables you to describe, explain and request whatever it is that can help shift this 'feeling'. The model comes from Dr David Rock (for more information see Sources and Further

Reading). As mentioned before, your brain is assessing your situations constantly. It's basically checking, 'Am I okay? Will I be okay? Is this, okay?' Rock's model is called SCARF and it invites you to consider five areas, to help you to work out what you need to know, in order to get back to being 'okay'.

This model can help with understanding your reactions under pressure in terms of the 4Cs of concept 1. I'll explain how later.

SCARF explores whether a situation is deemed a threat or an opportunity, in terms of your social brain needs. It can be immensely useful for leaders who are having negative feelings about a situation. The SCARF model can help to analyse which parts of a person's needs are not being satisfactorily met.

SCARF describes how your brain is unconsciously and continuously checking for threats (situations to withdraw from – AWAY response) and rewards (situations you are drawn to – TOWARD response)

SCARF model – Brain imaging shows brain activity related to perceived threats (adrenaline, cortisol is released) or rewards (dopamine, oxytocin, serotonin is released) in situations where these five SCARF areas are impacted.

- **Status** - We are wired to assess our value to

others, including looking for mutual respect. This impacts our perception of our self-esteem

- **Certainty** - What we don't know, we guess or anticipate and this can raise or lower our level of anxiety

- **Autonomy** - We assess our level of control and our options: do I have a say, am I being trusted, am I okay with the constraints?

- **Relatedness** – We're wired to find safety with others, so we assess: are you a friend or an 'enemy'?

- **Fairness** - We calculate levels of fairness in interactions, both personally and while observing how others are treated

Example

Take the example of having to give a presentation. If you feel ok about this, you'll likely respond in a 'toward' fashion. If you dread the idea, you likely react in an 'away' fashion.

A 'toward' reward response can look like:

S - 'This could help me show my knowledge'

C - 'I can do this'

A - 'I can do this how I want'

R - 'I'm okay with this audience'

F - 'It's my turn'

An 'away' threat response can look like:

S - 'I'll make a fool of myself'

C - 'I know I'll trip over words, as usual'

A - 'It doesn't feel like I have a choice how I do this'

R - 'Others might laugh or not turn up'

F - 'Why can't someone else do this?'

Working with leaders on particular situations about which they're concerned, this model helped us to look at the reasons for their feelings. We've been able to look at each SCARF element and find solutions or reframe the situation, helping them to choose the best action for them, rather than what might be easier or avoided.

SCARF can also help you when crafting messages to your team (or others). By considering the five scarf areas you can create a message that can address potential concerns.

Take a moment to review your leadership challenge/s from earlier in terms of the SCARF model

1. **What** aspects of your role as a leader or business owner put you under pressure?

2. **When** such a situation occurs what is your usual response?

What ideas does this model give you for addressing the situation? Are some or all of the SCARF elements (Status, Certainty, Autonomy, Relatedness, Fairness) standing out for your attention, reflection and action?

In conclusion

For leaders who are more naturally mentally tough, sometimes the optimism that everything is possible, will go well or will work out, doesn't always happen. On occasion, this can result in a drop in that leader's resilience and confidence, which can come as a shock to them and to others.

Steven Spielberg talks about how, after the massive success of *Close Encounters of the Third Kind,* he went through an incredibly low time when his later films were negatively criticised. His perception of his career, if explored through a SCARF lens, shows his optimism and self-belief had dipped and he talks about the courage he tapped into to get to get his future film successes.

These two concepts (4Cs and SCARF) work when you understand that courage is built through practising new ways, learning as you go, and having trusted people who encourage you.

With realistic optimism in the situations you face, and these two models, you can assess, plan and adjust to manage your mental toughness and courage and to implement great habits.

Reflection Space

This is your space to note further ideas and actions as a result of reading and taking part in this chapter.

Chapter 7
Leading with Courage During Challenging Times

What we, as individuals, find scary and requires courage is sometimes surprising to ourselves and others. Leading has many 'out of our comfort zone' moments. The leaders you and I admire are likely to be those who lean into the scary, saying what needs to be said and having a demeanour that gives you confidence in the toughest times.

I've been surprised when leaders have, for example, found it 'easier' to make a big announcement and implement the changes that this will require, rather than to let another team member know that their behaviour is not acceptable. Which would you find harder?

When your 'scary' is on the horizon you'll be fighting the desire to avoid it, ignore it and maybe run away from it. Leadership, especially authentic leadership, includes being scared. It's being alert to concerns and using that energy to focus and reason so that you can face what's required of you in a measured manner.

The phrase 'challenging times' means different things to different people.

You may draw on, or need, your courage when situations cause tension, fear and pressure. Often, although not always, these situations are surprises, things that you've not anticipated, or which are out of your control. Situations that can cause (negative) pressure and uncertainty. In leadership terms they can include:

- A takeover

- Competition

- A system or cyber issue

- Compliance or legal changes

- A drop in revenue or tight margins

- Global unrest

- People resourcing and performance matters

- A lack of product or the ability to produce

One or two challenges is one thing, but start adding personal matters into the mix and being courageous becomes a mindset to master. Those who have been dealing with 'challenges' for many years can find that one day it suddenly and surprisingly (to themselves and others) becomes 'too much'.

The issue here is that a level of self-awareness has been missing. In other words, the skill to understand oneself to a level that means that the warnings relating to (or the responses to) a sense of overwhelm are spotted, accepted and acted on.

Note also that it can take courage to admit to a sense of overwhelm.

Some neuroscience

A key player in raising your brain's anxiety level is uncertainty and surprises. For the brain to relax, and focus on managing your body's systems, it needs to have the answers to unanswered questions. Or it thinks it needs those answers. To help your brain to find solutions and calmness you will benefit from building your experience, trying new ways, testing your abilities and developing new skills and insights. Drawing on positive experiences (memories) increases your brain's ability, agility and optimism to 'find ways through' (resilience) a real or perceived challenge.

Example:

Take a high-pressure situation, such as a lifesaving operation. The lead surgeon is experienced and will have prepared, or have previous knowledge to draw on, as well as a team of other experts monitoring the patient or undertaking specific tasks. The operation will have an 'expected time' and considerations will be in place for things that could go wrong or be discovered that aren't yet known. With that experience and setup, the surgeon can carry out his or her role even more effectively, especially if two other elements (other than experience) are present.

The two additional elements are support (from the team around him or her, and others they can contact) and the length of time, the duration, in which the person needs to sustain their focus.

When an operation develops unexpected complications that disturb the duration, or the fail-safe planned for, the surgeon's ability to maintain clear thinking and apply his or her experience will be much more effective when they 'feel' supported.

A team that has confidence in each other's experience stays calmer for longer, ensuring the best possible decisions within their circumstances.

Experience, support and duration. When you are under pressure and know you are supported and, crucially, comfortable to draw on that support, anxieties and worries are reduced. Add in that you have an expected timescale and your brain relaxes as it knows that this 'risky' situation will end.

Being able to access support, and have known durations in pressured situations, enables people to be courageous and keep going.

Authentic courage as a leader includes sometimes feeling scared or inadequate; the important skill is to be able to recognise this and utilise that feeling, so that you can set up support and build ways to enable you to sustain your energy and clarity of thought. Staying 'strong' and not asking for or using support, can be the downfall of a leader.

Question: Who are your supporters? In Chapter 5 you had the opportunity to draw up a list of those you have trusted relationships with or could have. This list, along with others outside of work who you trust, provide you with prospects for possible support. And you for them. Remind yourself:

- Who you can confide in, and be open with. Also, who will help you question yourself?

- If you don't have supporters or trusted colleagues what more can you do to gain them?

- When have you had to keep going and be resilient when it felt hard, and what/who helped you to do that?

Question: As a leader of others, what kind of supporter are *you* being to your team, peers and others?

Question: What else can affect your courage and stamina in difficult times? Another look at the Bottom-Up, Outside-In, Top-Down (bio-psycho-social) model below from Chapter 2 can help here.

A three-way bio-psycho-social model
adapted from Sarah McKay PhD, *Brain Health for Dummies*

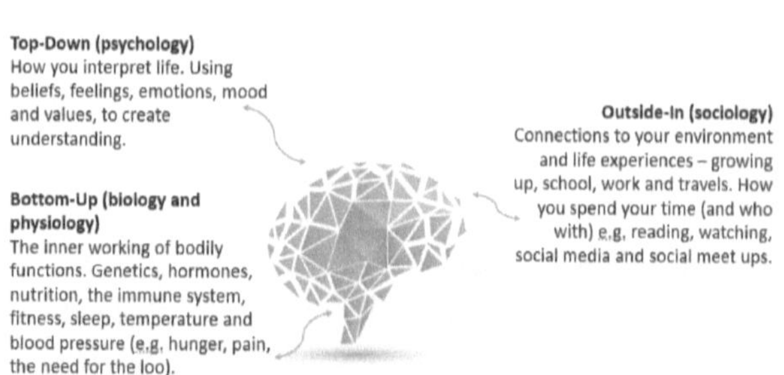

Perception about a situation can need checking.

Elements of the model above, in part, feed into your mindset in relation to challenges. Day by day, hour by hour, your biology, physiology, psychology and sociology influence how you lead. These elements need taking care of to aid your resilience in the face of difficulties.

Any situation is perceived based on:

- How you have interpreted life, which is feeding your unconscious and immediate reactions to situations (Top-Down)

- How you feel on a given day health-wise, which will steer your brain to direct resources where they will be most useful to your wellbeing. Logical processing won't necessarily be its priority if there are physiological concerns. In such circumstances, it can therefore be harder to focus and think clearly (Bottom-Up)

- The external stimuli that you connect with will be affecting your perceptions and ideas, and influencing your mood (Outside-In)

Did you know that the mood you wake up with steers how you perceive the world that day? Start your day in a good mood and you focus on what's going well and is positive. Start it in a bad mood, and your focus is drawn to what's wrong, unpleasant and negative. See the link to neuroscientist, Lisa Feldman Barrett's video in the bibliography. Lisa is an expert on how emotions are 'made' and explains brilliantly how your brain is wired in her book, *Seven and a Half Lessons about the Brain*.

Look back at Chapter 3 on emotions and moods. Recognising these and adjusting them as necessary can play a key part in reshaping your perception of challenges. This can help you to make more informed and logical choices and responses.

Have you ever been faced with a situation and reacted in horror to the idea?

Gaining the courage to move from a sense of threat to a sense of reward, builds your readiness for similar future situations. Remember, the more experiences you can build and learn from, the more expertise your brain has to assess with in future situations, and also be creative in how they are handled.

An idea. When something is daunting for you, aim to face it and be as effective as possible. This can mean putting the equation below into action.

Vulnerability + Acceptance = Courage

**(What you fear + openness in sharing
& expressing that fear = your first step into courage)**

It requires some effort and practice, plus support and empathy from a trusted person or coach who can help you to review your perceptions, maybe through the SCARF model (see Chapter 6), and examine the opportunities.

When anxiety surrounds a situation, it's important to be exposed (gently) to that 'threat' situation. With exposure, more certainty can be gained, which can lead to increased confidence in your abilities and options.

Importantly, have you noticed how, when you share a fear, others open up too? You connect on a human level. You can co-create amazing and supportive relationships with those you open up to, including your team, peers and those your report too.

Example

In Chapter 1, I mentioned how it took me ten years to accept my vulnerability and to share what I'd viewed as shameful parts of my life. When I accepted the vulnerability of potentially being judged negatively, and that I might face rejection because of my story, I found the courage to test out if my perception was true. But I'd been wrong... for years!

As soon as I told my story, people showed understanding, shared similar experiences and were interested to learn from my experience. I soon discovered that my vulnerability was to become a strength. It became an experience that I could use to assist leaders, managers and business owners to be more authentic, and in much less time than a decade. Find your supporters, keep them close and share your true feelings.

Idea: Anticipation helps to reduce uncertainty

Here's an idea that can help you to pre-empt situations you dread and helps you to plan in advance. Preparing for the situations you know can be stressful or that you dread (which may seem insignificant to others, because we're all different) helps to calm your mind should that scenario crop up, because you've solved it already!

Below is an example of how you could do this using an 'If/Then' approach.

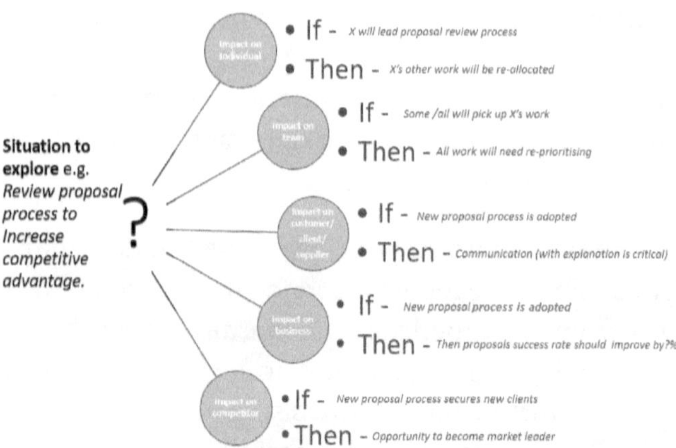

This model (above) aims to map the consequences of actions taken or not taken around an idea, problem, event or issue.

It informs choices and widens your awareness.

The phrases in the circles can be customised to suit the question being explored.

'If' captures thinking as it relates to each circle's heading and the main theme of the mapping.

'Then' captures a 'what next' dependent on the 'If'.

To conclude

Courage and resilience in leadership arrive with exposure, support and practice. Accepting your vulnerabilities, and being able to express them professionally, so that you can gain support, is part of you being you and gives you the opportunity to be authentically courageous.

The more you can share your concerns and test them (and yourself) out within 'sensible' parameters, the more certainty you will build in your abilities. Initially, emotions will often urge you to avoid situations, yet with a little more time and consideration, and by creating a plan such as the If/Then approach, fears can be much reduced or mitigated.

Brains love plans because, to the brain, anticipating and practising are the same as doing. This visualising and planning creates a new reference point to draw on, which reduces the surprises that can trigger a panic response.

Additional Bonus Material. You may want to test out some situations using the scaling techniques below (emotional or numerical) to see what you find challenging.

Pick a topic or situation that you need to address, but which you're not dealing with (yet).

Scale 1: Rate how difficult this situation seems to be: Easy, Medium, Hard, Very Hard, Expert.

- Whatever you select, what do you think you need, for you to be able to address this?

- What if you did nothing? How would that impact you and others, directly or indirectly?

Your knowledge and *capability* (it's one thing having the knowledge and another having the skill to apply that knowledge) and experience are critical in assessing how tough something is for you to deal with.

Scale 2: If you prefer numbers, you could scale challenges in terms of complexity and effort levels.

Lower levels (1–3): Quick wins and routine tasks

Mid-range (4–7): Tasks that require planning, perseverance and learning new skills

Upper range (8–10): Tasks that stretch or test your limits, often with high levels of uncertainty or risk

- Whatever you select, what do you think you need

for you to be able to address this?

- What if you did nothing? How would that impact you and others, directly or indirectly?

Your self-perception: the generated stories that you've been running throughout life create mind talk, that highlights your beliefs and values and which can be useful, or can clutter your clarity.

Scale 3: What if we expanded the assessment scale idea?

Trivial, Simple, Manageable, Demanding, Challenging, Complex, Difficult, Daunting, Overwhelming, Formidable

- Whatever you select, what do you think you need for you to be able to address this?

- What if you did nothing? How would that impact you and others, directly or indirectly?

Finally:

- What can you see more clearly through applying one or all of these scales, to how a situation is perceived (mental, emotional, physical and logistical demands)?

- How could the models discussed also support your team (or not)?

Reflection space

This is your space to note your ideas and actions as a result of reading and taking part in this chapter.

Chapter 8
Team Culture: a community of minds

Growing, tending, caring and nurturing are the themes that come up if you research the term 'culture'. This chapter is about consciously creating and being aware of the culture of your team as it changes and evolves. We'll explore leading with behaviours and structures that stimulate and maintain a positive culture. We'll also look at being explicit for all members of a team as to what's acceptable, and also unacceptable. Culture is impacted by your leadership style; we will touch on this too.

The neuroscience

A culture that creates a sense of being cared for is naturally attractive and directly linked to every person's need to belong. From your earliest moments, and without speech capabilities, you attempted to have your biological needs met by connecting with others. You did this through crying, smiling, laughing and being incredibly cute.

Those youngsters who've had secure and positive relationships are found to develop mentally and emotionally in a healthier way than those who, unfortunately, didn't. When, as an adult, you 'feel' neglected or less important, your brain's threat systems are triggered.

A brain chemical associated with belonging is oxytocin. It's directly linked to relationships that create feelings of care. Have you noticed how you smile when you think of people you care about or who care about you? This is oxytocin being triggered in recognition of that thought. Such relationships can reduce stress responses, and these can be vital for your team due to the pressures that can occur in a workplace.

Did you know that brains co-regulate each other? When you are (including virtually) with others who are, for instance, calm, your breathing will unconsciously synchronise with theirs. Your heart rate will too. Equally, matching occurs when tensions arise, causing an increase in breathing and heart rate.

The environments that you're a part of, if calm, supportive and joyous most of the time, enable each person to be more empathic, and are bodily and psychologically healthier, because of the co-regulation that is set off.

Where an extended sense of disconnection or loneliness exists (which is not about being on one's own - you can feel lonely in a relationship or group), this can increase sickness and lead to a decline in mental wellbeing as others aren't in place to assist appropriately with co-regulation.

Because feeling disconnected creates stress, your brain diverts its processes to look after your safety. Adrenalin and cortisol increase in readiness to protect you. This leads to other bodily functions being deprioritised, which can result in sickness.

Have you noticed how, when stressed, your digestive system can suffer, or your sleep becomes interrupted? Feeling alone or disconnected triggers bodily stress responses. Connection with others and caring, empathic conversations, can lead to a worried person's heart rate and breathing becoming calmer. Which allows the brain to redistribute resources in a balanced fashion, so reducing the chances of sickness or inflammation.

Toxic cultures result in increased sickness and absence!

You can find heaps more on brain health in *Brain Health for Dummies* by the neuroscientist that I studied with, Dr Sarah McKay and in the work of Lisa Feldman Barrett (see Sources and Further Reading section).

Exercise

List here the times you gather and connect with other people *and* feel like you belong.

Include both work and non-work gatherings.

** *e.g. Watching your favourite band*

**

**

**

**

** e.g. *At a work weekly catch-up session*

**

**

**

**

Questions

- What have you come up with?

- And, crucially, what gatherings are not on the list, because you don't feel connected? What is it about these other gatherings that causes discomfort for you?

You can refer to Chapters 6 and 7 and the SCARF model to help with revealing what you can do to understand and change this.

Your team is a social community, where your leadership can enable everyone to feel that they're part of that community. This sense of togetherness can raise individual and group productivity and wellbeing.

The previous chapters examine how to be, and assist you in being, a leader who can be authentic, genuine and courageous when needed. Your team's culture (the habits it cultivates, practises and grows) reflect directly on how you are leading, or not.

Example

This is what one of my clients told me about a leader in their organisation.

'He was a bully but charmed and blinded the top team with his charts and gizmos. I can't tell you how many people he was rude to, ridiculed and took their ideas as their [his] own. How do these smart people at the top not see what we see?'

Question

If someone in *your* business or organisation had the same negative perspective as the team member above, what would you suggest needed to be done?

The response to this kind of scenario influences the culture. The phrase 'behaviour breeds behaviour' comes to mind. If a culture is seen as a living thing, sometimes weeds will grow and go wild unless spotted and treated or prevented.

Creating the culture

I remember a time when a CEO sent a message to the whole organisation stating what the company's culture was. I messaged him privately saying that, in my opinion, a culture is an ongoing and fluid entity. It will differ depending on who is in charge and their behaviour. It can vary from one floor or office to another. It is fragile, especially when not everyone feels part of it, is accountable for it and, regardless of 'rank', has permission to hold others to it.

A way to create/assess your team's culture

You can start by putting the word 'care' in the centre as a cultural guide and then provide more clarity on what this might mean for you and the team, and what your organisation cares about.

Interpreting 'care' within the workplace, can look like:

- Tending to the needs of others, such as their opportunities and development

- Protecting yourself, others or a principle e.g. wellbeing, legalities and safety, including psychological safety

- Being attentive to, and acting prudently towards, what is happening, ways of working and others' opinions, as well as the results and outcomes

The above links to this model below (adapted from John Adair's idea of action-centred leadership), which illustrates the need to provide equal attention and care to each of three areas, so helping leaders to manage, lead and motivate their teams effectively.

The Three Lenses for Leadership

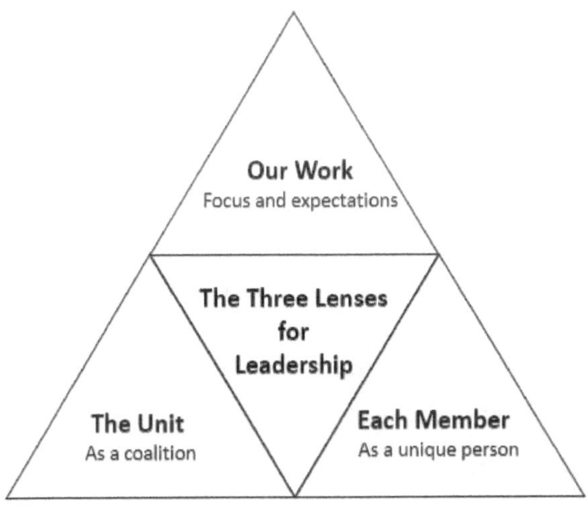

The Three Lenses for leadership is a concept that looks at:

- **Our Work** – Organising the work with clarity, precision and purpose (what, why, how, who, when)

- **Each Member** – Connecting with and understanding each team member's uniqueness, skills, motivations, knowledge and opportunities

- **The Unit** – Establishing an environment with the team as a unit that enables collaboration, and where each person cares about each other, to gain the best outcomes, in the best way, for all members and for the realisation of the team's goals

Example:

Imagine a juggler with three bean bags. Each bean bag represents one of the Three Lenses for Leadership. Juggling to keep all three bean bags in the air takes equal attention. If there's a dip in attention and one bean bag drops, often the other two will also.

Leading involves lots of juggling, apportioning your time appropriately across the Three Lenses for Leadership. It means prioritising but also not compromising on giving time to each area.

Creating a culture - Below is an idea for co-creating with your team (the unit) the culture that will best serve them all.

Idea! Connecting minds and creating the culture – Your team's charter

Here is a template – including satellites surrounding the team – which helps everyone to identify how you and they care for the work and for each other.

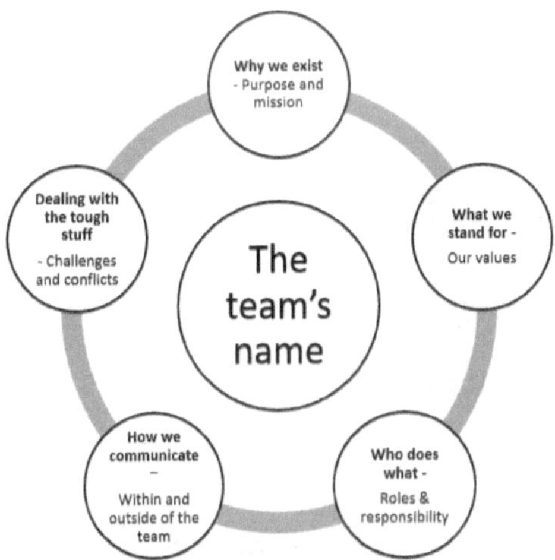

Here's a nine-step team charter process for you and your team to co-create, review and refresh. This establishes the guidelines for your team's culture and acts as its compass.

1. Make sure that this is a whole group activity – and get the agreement of the team

2. Share the template as is, or adapt to suit

3. While waiting for feedback, and afterwards if needed, prepare prompting questions to go with each of the satellites surrounding the team's name

4. Brainstorm the questions and answers with the group, adding questions if necessary, and also checking that you have the appropriate number of satellites (you may find the need to add a topic)

5. Synthesise (gather together) the outcomes

6. Draft a charter

7. Listen to feedback and comments

8. Establish agreement and commitment

9. Agree the next review date

What, why and how for each step:

1. Ensure that this is a whole group activity. For inclusivity, effective collaboration and to generate and maintain commitment, it's important to include all team members.

2. Share the template for initial feedback on the idea of a charter to support a positive culture, including the satellite elements it could contain. This could be done in person, virtually or by email.

3. While waiting for feedback, and afterwards if needed, prepare prompting questions for each satellite. These will be used to collate thoughts and co-create what the group's shared charter will contain. Here are some example prompts for each satellite. How the team answers can highlight all sorts of areas that need acknowledgement and further clarification.

Why we exist – questions

- Why does our team exist?

- What if this team didn't exist?

- How do we impact the company's vision/mission?

- Our goals as a team this year are…?

- How are our processes and standards helping or hindering?

What we stand for – questions

- What do we want to be known for, what's our vision?

- What are our values as a team? See Chapter 4 for a values list.

- What do we want being in this team to 'feel' like?

- What will we not stand for?

- Is there a behaviour/behaviours we want to prioritise (e.g. openness, reflection)?

Who does what – questions

- Who leads on what? How are we being kept accountable?

- Who supports these people and how?

- What is expected of each of our roles (goals, objectives, timelines)?

- How are we linking our values to the way we carry out our roles?

How we communicate – questions

- What ways will we stay connected with each other, in person and virtually?

- Who will communicate what and when and how, externally?

- How and how often will we meet? For how long?

- Do we require time boundaries for when we contact each other?

- What and how will we celebrate, internally and externally?

Dealing with the tough stuff – questions

- How will we be expected to respond when we are challenged or questioned by a fellow team member?

- How is conflict or disagreement from an external source to be dealt with?

- In what ways can we indicate that we need help?

- When unplanned events occur (unexpected absences, a change in requirements, restructures), how will we support each other, practically and emotionally?

- How will we rate difficulties to know when to escalate them?

4. Brainstorm the questions and answers with the group, either in person or virtually. Here are some ways to do this:

- **In person** – Be creative in how information is shared and captured. So, for example, have large Post-its and colourful pens as well as an inspiring space with ample room, music and perhaps snacks

- **Virtual** – See www.mentimeter.com – an online tool which allows interaction, with virtual Post-its, votes, word cloud generation, etc

- **Options** – Take each satellite and work through it together, or split the team into sub-groups and give each a satellite, a length of time (e.g. 45 minutes) and the expectation of sharing, explaining and accepting feedback (e.g. 30 minutes)

- **Timing** – You could dedicate one day to brainstorming all the satellites or choose to do a number of satellites within a specific time frame

- **If everyone can't attend** – ensure they all contribute to the group session outputs and have the opportunity to question and to add information – speaking to them, rather than just emailing or messaging.

- **Use tools such as Teams** to capture the overall process and collate the stages/information so all can easily access progress.

5. Synthesise the outcomes into a first draft charter. I'd recommend that you, as the leader of the team, do this. When drafting:

- Get specific and give clarity to each of the charter satellites

- Include metrics and timings so expectations are clear and people know what they're agreeing to

Then circulate it to the team for their additions, questions and afterthoughts.

6. Following feedback, draft an updated charter – and share it. Be creative, use images, quotes, icons and inspiring language.

7. Listen to the feedback and comments. Talk to the team individually to get your best understanding of people's views. Make necessary adjustments.

8. Establish agreement and commitment. Once adjustments have been made (if needed), launch the charter and keep referring to it as the main guide for you as the leader, and for the team. Use it for onboarding too.

9. Set a regular review date. To keep the charter relevant and of value it needs tending to.

Through this charter, your culture has been co-defined and co-designed – now what?

This process reveals much about how things are now and how they can be even better for your team.

It can highlight changes needed in all areas of the Three Lenses for Leadership model (again, see below), informing on process, communication, behaviours and the team's overarching and individual goals. Also, on leadership styles for you to adopt.

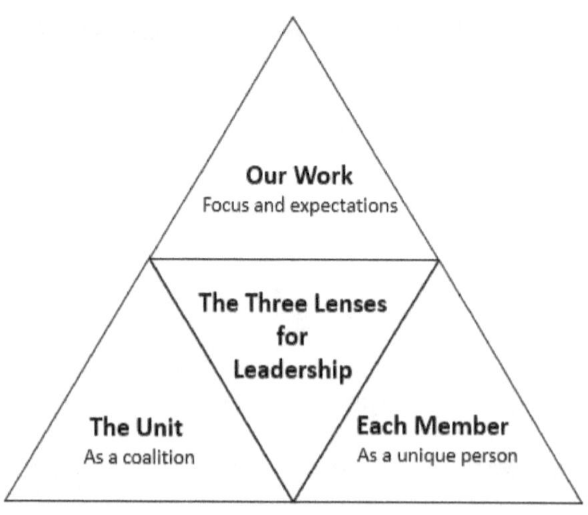

The changes your charter may cause for you as a leader

When roles, responsibilities, boundaries, authority levels, values and expectations are set, you may well find that you have to adjust how you've been leading. The next chapter looks at two areas of leading that leaders I have worked with can find challenging: delegating and giving feedback.

To conclude

Committing fully to cultivating and maintaining a caring and productive team culture can require courage from both you and your team. A question in the prompts under communication: 'What and how will we celebrate, internally and externally?' is by no means frivolous. This question is a tool for you as a leader to recognise the effort and commitment that shows up. It allows you and others to encourage and support the continued application of a positive and caring team culture.

Reflection space

What will you do next to increase your understanding of your team's culture and develop it?

Chapter 9
Leading Authentically: delegation and feedback

Many leaders and business owners struggle with delegating, and the giving or receiving of feedback. These skills and a leader's relationship with them will impact the team's performance and its culture.

In this chapter you'll see some ways to think about and execute these two skills, with a reference to four different leadership styles, of which delegation is one. Where there is fear or dread attached to these activities I recommend going back to chapters in the book that give insight into your values and beliefs, and to understanding emotions, and to use these to guide you in dealing with situations in a way that is authentic for you as a responsible leader.

About Delegation

Example

One of my clients expressed that they had sleepless nights worrying that a person they had delegated too would mess up. So they kept checking the person's work and then correcting it and, in so doing, doubled their own workload. The fact is, they hadn't actually delegated!

This leader's own fear of failing was being transferred to their team member. I suggested they look at allocating work in terms of risk – what was at risk? We also explored this from the angle of learning and how mistakes are often where we learn the most.

We looked at the difference between 'saving people' and being available to advise and give them a sense of autonomy and responsibility. We also compared what that leader was being paid to do, with what the role holder was being paid to do.

What/how to delegate – it's important to know what your leadership role alone is responsible for. These are areas which can't be delegated. Often that will include things such as budget decisions over a certain amount, performance evaluations for your direct reports, access to some company information, etc. It's important to know these and confirm them if you're in doubt.

Everything else is an opportunity for delegation, with clear expectations and timelines, and possibly an opportunity for a team member's development. When delegating, the work has to go to the right person, the individual or individuals with the relevant skills, knowledge and motivation. **The Three Lenses for Leadership model:** 'Our Work, Each Member, The Unit' introduced in Chapter 8, when given regular time too, helps you to know more quickly who a suitable person is to delegate too.

Delegation and the assignment of work is task specific. It's the process of matching the task with the best person to do it. This does not mean the most willing person, or the one with the least on their plate. Sometimes, delegating a task to the best person means having to reassign something else they do to another team member.

You should only delegate if the person the work is to be allocated to has the relevant skills and motivation. Which means you KNOW you can let them be self-directive in how they fulfil that task.

Tip – if delegating means that certain people will no longer be interacting with you, make their new contact point aware of this, and reassure them of your belief in, and of the competence of, the person they will now be liaising with. I also recommend introducing them to that person and doing a handover.

Delegating still requires you to be the assessor of your team's performance and to check in on the person or persons' progress and the quality of their work. However, the frequency of doing so can be less often.

Alternative leadership styles to delegating

Delegating is one style of leading and one that is not always appropriate. If someone doesn't have the exact skills, or the motivation, a different leadership style should be adopted.

When a capable person is less enthusiastic to take on a task, a **'Selling'** style can be adopted. This can be useful with someone you recognise to be capable and who would gain from the experience. Selling can include aspects such as career development, an opportunity for the person to expand their impact and increase their exposure in the organisation, and as recognition of their growing abilities.

Sometimes an ideal person is willing and able but lacks confidence or self-belief. In this situation, applying a **'Coaching or Participating'** style requires you to be a little more hands-on, leading from the sidelines. Participating involves hearing their ideas and thoughts about getting the task done and encouraging them to test and learn. It can include reminding them of, or having them recall, other successes, and connecting these to the task they are being given trust to take on.

Where there is little experience, but the task is relevant to their role, a '**Tell**' approach with a '**Directing**' style is best. This can include giving clear, step-by-step instructions, processes to follow, and timelines and involves close observation.

However, as a person gains in skill and confidence, this style can become frustrating and should be shifted to a **Coaching** style (or a **Selling** one, if needed), before moving to a full delegating approach.

Tip – with any of these styles, sharing how *you* have progressed and how *you* have had to overcome your own doubts and challenges reveals your humanness, your authentic self.

Sometimes there isn't anyone to delegate to, even if the task distracts you from more valuable parts of your role. It's one of the pressures that many leaders come up against. In this scenario, here are some suggestions:

- Recheck your priorities within the work schedule, prioritising what is the most valuable use of your time, linked to yours and the organisations objectives

- Filter the meetings you attend – only go to those where there's a clear reason for you to do so, and value in attending. You might not have to stay for the whole meeting

- Reduce the duration of meetings

- Keep your energy (and rest) in balance

- Remember that connecting on a human level with your team, as a whole and individually, is always valuable time, even when you are stretched

- And, if drastic change is needed, prepare a business case with solutions to address the matter:

  ○ Cost efficiencies that would come from your proposals

  ○ Process checks, a review of tasks and overlaps with other teams

  ○ A restructure – adjusting roles and responsibilities

  ○ An IT system enhancement

Want to learn more about leadership styles? The idea above (identifying the best leadership style for each situation) relates to 'Situational Leadership' and The Centre for Leadership Studies, as referenced in Sources and Further Reading. Four styles have been mentioned:

Leadership style	Appropriate use
Delegating	Where the person has experience and they don't need supervising
Selling	Where a team member has experience but can't see the value to themselves
Coaching/participating	Where there are transferable skills, but confidence might not be so high
Directing (or telling)	Where the team member is inexperienced (and possibly overconfident)

Idea

Go through your daily tasks/responsibilities and earmark those that would be appropriate to delegate, if the right person/role were available.

This insight can be used to inform proposals for structural change, recruitment criteria and training and development opportunities. It can also enable you to create space for your own development.

About Feedback

Authentic leadership requires honesty, not just with yourself, but with those you interact with. Referring to the previous chapter on culture: positive cultures include two-way dialogue.

Example

In the past, when very new to leading, I didn't always address the whole situation. Sometimes I drifted around the edges, hoping my hints would be noticed and changes adopted. I'd end up silently frustrated with myself.

I learnt to handle this by getting closer to what I admire in leaders and emulating those I respected. A phrase I now share with my clients comes from Brené Brown, author of *Dare to Lead*.

'Clear is kind, unclear is unkind.'

With this quote at the centre of your preparation, all feedback, the good, the bad and the ugly, can be handled with grace.

Example

A passionate, approachable and caring leader I coached rarely drew the line. Chance after chance was given to a team member's disappointing performance.

The situation had arisen due to the team member suffering from stress within their usual role. To support them, a less stressful role was carved out. This still required regular attendance at work, and attention to detail, although less customer interaction.

The team member (A) was however, still regularly absent. The consequence being that their work was then taken on by another team member (B), and the leader, by subsequently supporting (B), was also picking up additional tasks.

'Clear is kind, unclear is unkind.'

Team member A needed some feedback on their performance and a discussion about their abilities at this time. The leader was understandably hesitant to address this, although they could see that team member B's work, and their own, was going to suffer if things continued as they were. To help craft the right approach to this we explored the situation through Brené Brown's quote (above) on kindness: in this case, kindness to A and to all those impacted by the current arrangement.

- How is keeping someone in a role that requires more regular attendance, or the application of skills that they aren't currently achieving (and may not be able to) kind to them and to the others affected?

- What would be kinder to them and to the others affected?

- Outside of this current role, what other options are possible and what is off the table at this time? Consult with HR experts for the latest best practice and policy.

Preparing to give feedback

To identify both positives and negatives, link your feedback to the Three Lenses for Leadership model (Our Work, Each Member, The Unit). Also to the values of the organisation and the team, the team's charter, and the organisation's vision and strategy.

Ask yourself:

- What impact is this person's behaviour, actions and results having on the **Our work** their role requires?

- How do you know you've been clear on what is expected regarding their work and how they conduct themselves?

- If you asked them to describe what is expected of them from their work, how will they answer?

- What impact are they having on **The Unit** they are a part of?

- How are they helping or hindering the relationships and productivity of others in and outside of the team?

- What behaviours and responsibilities have **The Unit** to each other? If you have a charter, you have a great tool to refer to.

- What impact are they having on themselves (**Each Member**), including their reputation, progress, opportunities for development or career choices?

Idea for mindset

Remind yourself about having a listening mindset (Chapter 5). Your observations or questions can provide you with feedback or previously unknown information. In some cases, this may or should shift your previously held perception. Remember that your mindset will impact the outcome of any conversation, especially in relation to how you want people to think and feel as a result.

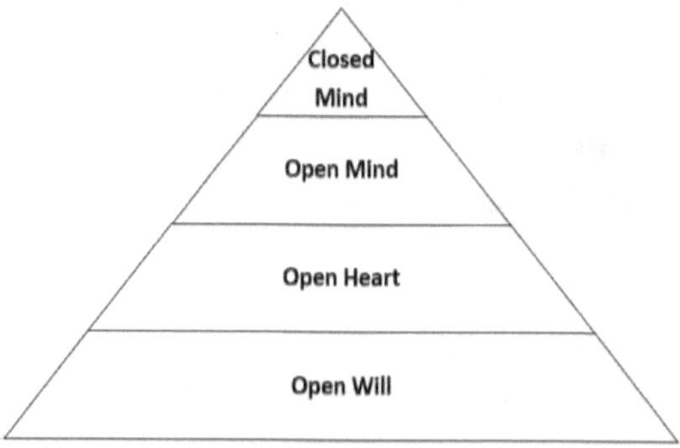

Some find that giving feedback makes them feel nervous. Giving or receiving feedback creates many emotional responses. Managing these is crucial in supporting a healthy culture and in maintaining an open mindset. The chapter on emotions (Chapter 3) is there to support you in choosing the best emotional mindset for a healthy and professional conversation.

In summary

Rarely in life is there a 'one-size' fits all solution. Leading is no different. People's lives and needs evolve, sometimes on a daily basis. Self-awareness regarding your own state is important, as it will influence your leadership behaviour and outcomes. Frameworks, as shown here and in other chapters help give structure to how you prepare for and address your leadership situations. Emotional management helps you to apply them well.

Aim to pick your emotional state and your leadership style consciously.

Reflection space

Ask yourself, in given situations or with certain people:

- Who am I being?

- Am I being clear and kind, with the good and not so good information?

- Am I addressing what needs to be addressed?

- Am I preparing so that I can behave as the leader I would admire?

Chapter 10
Being Your Own Leadership Coach

I've written a lot about valuing the support of others and how important it is to have people around you, helping you and you helping them.

The downside is that you can become reliant on others and sometimes no one is available to you. Self-confidence and self-reliance are key to a leader's mental toughness and resilience in difficult times.

We've all had that time in the middle of the night, when you're wide awake and frantic about a situation and it's not a suitable time to contact anyone. You can lie there worrying or perhaps distract yourself with a podcast or meditation. Lying in bed is not restful, so it can be useful to get up, to move a bit, rehydrate, make a few notes and maybe quietly try this self-coaching method (you can do this at any time of day).

The idea comes from a webinar on group coaching, hosted by Haesun Moon PhD, author of *Coaching A-Z*, and an expert in the power of language. Moon's research shows how by using careful prompts you can focus your mind on progressing to solutions.

The self-coaching approach below that I'm sharing requires you to read or say the questions to yourself. It should not take more than about 10 minutes.

Example: In the group coaching session mentioned above, this online group of unconnected people were all asked a number of questions like those below. Everyone was asked to write down their answers. No one spoke while doing this and no one shared what was on their mind. Everyone worked independently. Each question led our thinking and ideas and drew us to past successes and future desires. It highlighted what could be reapplied and was useful in progressing to a positive outcome.

When we'd finished, everyone indicated (and some shared in more detail) that they had indeed made progress with 'what was on their mind'. Including myself.

As a language expert, Moon highlighted that by using the phrase, 'What's on your mind?' this doesn't infer that the issue is necessarily negative – which words or phrases such as 'problem' or 'need help with' can infer. Instead, it's a neutral phrase influencing your mind away from defensiveness.

An example of how this works

Here are thirteen thought prompts (the number and the questions may vary). The responses below in italics are from a case study (using this method), with a coachee of mine.

1. **Write down what is on your mind, i.e. a recurring or a currently frequent thought.**
   It's about a team member I don't like, they focus on negatives, complain and it drains my energy.

2. **What makes this important?**
   They irritate me – I want to avoid them. I shouldn't, and probably I don't make time for them because of it. It's not good leadership on my part.

3. **How can focusing on this for a while make a positive difference for you?**
   It can unstick me, give me another way of dealing with this.

4. **When have you worked through something similar before?**
   There have been a few times when I've had to mix with people I don't gel with. On occasion, I've been able to avoid them. One time, I had an issue with a neighbour (I'd just moved in) so I bit the bullet, invited them in and we chatted over a beer. We

both learnt a lot about each other, and it resulted in us being more friendly. This was fortunate, as I know people with horrific neighbour situations, so handling this quickly seemed to make sense. It was nerve racking though – it might not have worked.

5. **What small change/s can you make from now onwards that would make a positive difference to what's on your mind?**
   I could call the team member and ask them how they are as, lately, they seem more frustrated.

6. **What else could that small change do for you?**
   It could help me connect in a different way, and potentially understand them better, and show them that I'm trying to understand them.

7. **By doing this, what would other people notice about you?**
   They might notice less tension in me at the mention of, and in the presence of, this person.

8. **How will this impact relationships associated with 'What's on your mind?' and beyond?**
   It could increase trust between me and this person. It could also create relief in others.

9. **How would you rate this situation currently – 0 (changing this is a fantasy) to 10 (it's happening in parts already)?**
   I'd rate this as a 5.

10. **What would be a 'good enough' rating if 10 was not about perfection but 'most of the time'?**

    A good enough rating would be an 8-9.

11. **Why have you chosen this score and how would you maintain it?**

    Because my aim is for the person and I to have professional relationships, not just with me but with others too, most of the time. I'd maintain the score with a more regular check-in, clearer expectations, encouraging the behaviour that has improved, and exploring the situation with less judgement when it hasn't.

12. **What have you discovered from this exploration? Any surprises or new thinking?**

    I've discovered that I've had similar situations happen before and avoiding them isn't the answer. Facing this is good for many, not just for me.

13. **If those who knew about this situation met you in a couple of weeks' time, what would you want them to now ask or say about it?**

    Whether I've noticed (or they have noticed) that the person concerned has changed and is more pleasant to work with. What caused the change?

Your go!

A tip – give yourself about 30 seconds to answer each question. You can always revisit your answers another day and see how your responses/ideas have changed.

To Conclude

Not everyone has access to a leadership coach, although you know where I am when you need assistance. This approach allows you to access your own inner coach. Moving forwards with your findings, having used this technique, can increase self-trust and confidence in dealing with subsequent troublesome thoughts and situations. It helps to build 'mentally tough' behaviours. You also have the guidance and tips from previous chapters to assist you with your thoughts on how best to act.

This is also a great way for leaders to work with their teams on group solutions – collating the ideas discovered from the prompts (which can be reshaped), or with individual team members who are in your care.

Reflection space

What ideas are coming up for you as a result of reading this chapter and taking part in this exercise?

Conclusion and What Next

At the start, in the introduction, I suggest that you are always authentic. Further on, you discover that how you act and respond to your leadership role (and life) is based on how a belief about a situation, and your values, stimulates your feelings about it.

What you believe and value is directly influencing your thoughts (inner voice), feelings and behaviours. If all you do because of this book is to gain awareness and greater consciousness of your mind's perspective on yourself and your life's experiences, you will have increased your potential for being an even better leader with others.

If you go on to explore these often-age-old beliefs, challenge them, update them or reduce their importance, your identity as a leader and your way of leading will change with you. As you become clearer and more certain on what you stand for, it's hard to keep it hidden. The mask that comes with fear, dread or other less positive emotions is no longer needed.

Your true leadership identity shines through. Courage comes from discovering this identity and, when you have, so does the confidence to be a better form of authenticity. You are more confident and can hold your head up. How will this look?

If you don't know – you'll ask, if you're a bit fearful – you'll share that and if you're overwhelmed, you'll take a break to regain balance. If you're wrong – you'll take responsibility and if you're challenged, you'll listen. If you're scared – you'll not rush to push that feeling away and if you're confident and others are not, you'll notice and take the time to understand them.

No one is infallible (least of all me). There will be days when honesty and being you at your best is hard. The courage to speak your mind may be more daunting and take more effort or energy. You might be challenged and maybe don't handle that so well. A sense of not being good enough creeps in. When that happens, revisit the chapters in this book that focus on your values, or check back in with your beliefs as to what a good leader is, reset, and BE THAT LEADER!

My last idea – keep a journal of your achievements and milestones, big or small – things you've done or overcome. Appreciate your own efforts, despite the setbacks. This exercise builds credits in your mind and memory. The more credits you have and can draw on, the easier it is to avoid unhelpful mind talk and feelings. Re-read it often.

It reinforces your confidence and positivity for future challenges.

This journalling process helps you to be your own cheerleader. It can assist you in being less sensitive at times when others might not be there to boost your morale..

What next

If you've recognised yourself – or your team – in these pages, you may find that the most meaningful progress happens in dialogue. Working directly with the me offers a space to personalise the insights, explore your patterns, and create change that sticks. Lets talk!

My contact details: dominique@head4leadership.co.uk

Sources and Further Reading

Acas (2005). *Colleagues not doing jobs properly makes staff angriest at work* [Results of a YouGov PLC poll commissioned by Acas]. Available at: www.acas.org.uk/colleagues-not-doing-jobs-properly-ma kes-staff-angriest-at-work

Barrett, L. Feldman (2021). *Seven and a half lessons about the brain.* New York: Mariner Books.

Barrett, L. Feldman (2024). *Your mood influences what you see and hear (part 1).* Available at: youtu.be/-1mc9xOhGXw?si=wW0Z6gVrQVoAx4CB

Barron, H. C., et al. (2020). 'Neuronal Computation Underlying Inferential Reasoning in Humans and Mice', *Cell*, 183(1), pp.228-243. Available at: https://www.doi.org/10.1016/j.cell.2020.08.035

BiteSize Learning (2024). *The SCARF model of social threat & reward: the SCARF model, explained.* Available at: https://www.bitesizelearning.co.uk/resources/scarf-mod el-david-rock-explained

Brown, B. (2018). *Clear Is Kind. Unclear Is Unkind.* Available at: brenebrown.com/articles/2018/10/15/clear-is-kind-uncl ear-is-unkind

Cambridge Dictionary (2019). 'Conversation' [its meaning in the Cambridge (English) Dictionary]. Available at: dictionary.cambridge.org/dictionary/english/conversatio n

Clough, P., et al. (2021). *Developing Mental Toughness: strategies to improve performance, resilience and wellbeing in individuals and organizations.* 3rd edn. Kogan Page.

Coyle, D. (2018). *The Culture Code.* Random House.

Edmondson, A. C. and Mortensen, M. (2021). What Psychological Safety Looks Like in a Hybrid Workplace. *Harvard Business Review.* Available at: hbr.org/2021/04/what-psychological-safety-looks-like-in -a-hybrid-workplace

Forbes Business Council (2019). *16 Effective Ways to Encourage Strong Team Relationships*. Available at: https://www.forbes.com/councils/forbesbusinesscouncil /2019/12/26/16-effective-ways-to-encourage-strong-tea m-relationships

Galan, S. (2025) *Feeling of loneliness among adults 2021, by country.* Available at: https://www.statista.com/statistics/1222815/loneliness- among-adults-by-country/

Galford, R. M., et al. (2012). *The Trusted Advisor.* Simon & Schuster.

Goleman, D. (1998). *Working with Emotional Intelligence.* New York: Bantam Books.

Hoffman Institute UK (2019). *Feelings List.* Search online for: Hoffman Institute Feelings List.

Kirova, D. (2021). *How values shape identity.* Available at: values.institute/how-values-shape-identity

McKay, S. (2025). *Brain Health for Dummies.* John Wiley & Sons.

McKay, S. (2019). *Six brain-based solutions to beat stress.* Available at: https://www.drsarahmckay.com/six-brain-based-solution s-to-beat-stress

Moon, H. (2022). *Coaching A to Z: the extraordinary use of ordinary words.* Vancouver: Page Two Books.

NeuroLaunch (2024). *Emotion vs Feeling vs Mood: unraveling the psychological trio*. 18 Oct. 2024. Available at: https://www.neurolaunch.com/emotion-vs-feeling-vs-mood

Poutanen, E. (2018). *Understand Your social brain – The SCARF® Model*. 16 Aug. 2018. Available at: https://neuroleadership.fi/wp/blog/understand-your-social-brain-the-scarf-model/

Rock, D. and Cox, C. SCARF ® in 2012: updating the social neuroscience of collaborating with others. *NeuroLeadership Journal*, no. 4, 2012. Available at: https://www.academia.edu/25000956/SCARF_in_2012_updating_the_social_neuroscience_of_collaborating_with_others

Salovey, P. and Mayer, J. D. (1990). 'Emotional Intelligence', *Imagination, Cognition and Personality*, 9(3), pp.185–211. Available at: https://www.journals.sagepub.com/doi/10.2190/dugg-p24e-52wk-6cdg

Strycharczyk, D. and Perry, J. (2025). *Why We Need to Better Understand What We Mean by Strengths*. Available at: https://www.aqrinternational.co.uk/why-we-need-to-better-understand-what-we-mean-by-strengths

TalentLMS (2025). *Quiet Cracking: a hidden workplace crisis*. Available at: https://www.talentlms.com/research/quiet-cracking-workplace-survey

The Center for Leadership Studies (2020). *The Four Leadership Styles of Situational Leadership®*. Available at: https://www.situational.com/blog/the-four-leadership-styles-of-situational-leadership

Vuslat Foundation (2024). *Otto Scharmer's Four Levels of Listening: a journey to conversational depth*. Available at: https://www.generouslistening.org/otto-scharmers-four-levels-of-listening-a-journey-to-conversational-depth

Acknowledgements

Over time, I've had a few goes at writing a book that would accompany my work and demonstrate my passion for making leading and the leadership role feel more natural. While networking (@onle) one day I met my book coach Ellie Stevenson (Motivation to Publication *and beyond:* motivationtopublication.com). I got on with her, arranged a call – and off we set on this journey to my first book. The help she gave came in many ways – a warm and encouraging manner, a structured process, regular catchups and, in our case, a chapter a month. I wrote and Ellie fed back on how it made sense or not, including grammar and better ways to word things – you are gold dust, thank you!

Without all the people in my life: those I have lived with, worked with, am friends with and have learned with – without you, I wouldn't have been able to draw on some of the experiences shared in this book.

To those out there who have influenced me through your research and insights – my Sources and Further Reading section refers to just some of this learning more closely.

Your knowledge has opened my mind to so much. My gratitude to you is immense.

A massive thanks to those of you who have been part of the beta reads and who fed back their thoughts and perspectives – this has been greatly appreciated. A shout out to Eleanor Towsey – Director at a family law firm of solicitors, Stuart Bagnall – Communications Director at a UK university and Julie Woodward – Director in client education.

To my talented nephew Dan (insta @dan_coope.r), a graphic designer, who agreed to work with me on the cover, thank you!

To my husband Bob, my biggest cheerleader, who kept encouraging me and bringing me tea. I love you.

About the Author

Dominique Stillman is a leadership coach of twenty plus years who works with senior executives, business owners, senior leaders and new and aspiring managers through her coaching and team development business, Head 4 Leadership.

From age 19 she led businesses for ten years and then, after an economic downturn, had to start again – from the ground up. She worked hard, consistently applying herself to get back on her feet. Now, Dominique uses that experience, along with her resulting corporate journey (from contributor to new manager to global leadership role), in her coaching, team development and mentoring services. Along the way she has gained a multitude of coaching, personality assessment and other qualifications. Her studies in neuroscience and mental toughness have helped her make sense of how she got through her own tough times and are central to her work with leaders today.

Dominique's goal is to add to the number of healthy workplace cultures, cultures that are a result of leadership that is authentic and courageous, and also compassionate.

www.head4leadership.co.uk

https://www.linkedin.com/in/dominiquestillman